DOES
SIN MATTER?

Other Books by Frank O'Loughlin
published by Coventry Press

Gathering the People of God
New Wineskins: Eucharist in Today's Context

DOES
SIN MATTER?

Separation, Reconciliation, Redemption

FRANK O'LOUGHLIN

COVENTRY
PRESS

Published in Australia by
Coventry Press
33 Scoresby Road
Bayswater VIC 3153

ISBN 9781922589187

Scripture quotations are from *The Revised New Jerusalem Bible*, copyright © 2019 by Darton, Longman & Todd, Ltd and Doubleday, a division of Penguin Random House, Inc. Reprinted by Permission.

Catalogue-in-Publication entry is available from the National Library of Australia http://catalogue.nla.gov.au

Cover design by Ian James – www.jgd.com.au
Text design by Coventry Press
Set in Pagella 11.5 pt

Printed in Australia

To
Thomas Michael Doyle
who frequently urged me to write this book

To

Thomas Michael Doyle

who frequently urged me to write this book

Contents

Introduction

When I told people that I was intending to write a book on sin, I received many diverse reactions, some of which were quite dismissive of the project, while others were encouraging and even intrigued. Each of these reactions had the effect of reinforcing my intention to write the book; they confirmed my conviction that we need to change the way in which we speak about sin.

The suggestion for the book came from a priest friend of mine with long and varied experience of life in the Church. He urged me to write because he felt that there was a growing gap between the inherited understanding of sin and what made sense to the greater part of the people of the Church. He also felt that what was often said about sin did not measure up to the words and actions of Christ in the Gospels.

Discourse on sin within the Church often reflected a closed Catholic world that made less and less sense to those outside the Church. And even more importantly, this was also the case with so many of the people of God themselves who, of course, live the Christian life as participants in their contemporary society and culture.

In all matters, the Church has to be strongly rooted in the person of Christ in whom it finds its identity while at the same time being a community of people who are part of the world in which they live and in which they have their specific mission. The Church is called to be a community that is inviting and welcoming to people rather than a community closed in upon itself.

A crucial element of this openness is the language that is used in the Church. Language can be both a great bridge and a great barrier. If we use a language within the Church that is too tied to the past and unrelated to the contemporary situation, we will not be understood beyond the theologically educated members of the Church. We would be imprisoning the gospel in a language that is unable to communicate it.[1]

Our task today is the same as it has always been: how to express the faith in a new context, in a language that gives those who know nothing of the gospel a starting point from which to come to an appreciation of Christ. What the Church has to say has to be said in such a way that it is aware of the society in which it lives. We betray our mission by being closed in upon ourselves. As Pope Francis has frequently said, dialogue is the way ahead for the Church today.[2]

In proclaiming the gospel, we are presenting a mystery that is ultimately beyond us and so we cannot be simplistic in its presentation, nor can we presume that people are going to be drawn to it simply by our proclaiming it. It requires genuine dialogue and a respect for those with whom we live and communicate (see 1 Peter 3:13-16). We

---

[1] Pope Francis, *Evangelii Gaudium*, Strathfield, NSW: St Pauls Publications, 2013, no. 41.
[2] *Evangelii Gaudium*, 46-49.

also know that in every age this mystery has shown that it has the capacity to grasp and enthuse human beings. We also have to acknowledge that we are not in control of the word of God. Pope Francis speaks of 'the unruly freedom of the word, which accomplishes what it wills in ways that surpass our calculations and ways of thinking'.[3]

In being the Church today, one of the things we need to speak about is sin. There is an aspect of human life that is gradually revealed as 'sin' throughout the Scriptures and, most fully, in the life, death and resurrection of Jesus Christ.

The revelation of sin is an aspect of human relationship with God which comes to the surface in the history of God's covenant with Israel, recorded in the Old Testament books of the Bible and in that new covenant made in and through Christ, recorded in the New Testament books. The Scriptures make it clear that what we call sin is not part of the divinely created nature of the world; but rather is something that is not supposed to be there! It is a parasite on God's good world.

One of the points that will come up in this book is that evil/sin is an enigma. Thinkers of all kinds struggle to understand it; its source seems to be untraceable. One suggestion is that its source is so radically negative that it cannot be understood. One author suggests that not even God can understand it![4]

---

[3] *Evangelii Gaudium*, 22.

[4] Neil Ormerod, *Creation, Grace and Redemption*. Maryknoll, NY: Orbis Books, 2007, p. 17.

My hope is that, even at this early stage of the book, the reader is wondering what sin really means. This is my hope because, as the book goes on, I will be suggesting that all of us need to change our general thinking about sin.

The purpose of the book is to consider the question of sin with the help of the Scriptures, the Christian tradition, theologians and people who give voice to the questions and wonderings of our times.

Chapter 1

Has Thinking About Sin Changed?

Some pastoral issues give rise to and require a renewed *theological* understanding of the matter in hand. An understanding of and pastoral approach to human sinfulness is one such issue.

As a part of our starting point, we should take note of the fact that so few Catholics continue the practice of confessing their sins to a priest. Formerly, that practice was a significant thread in the makeup of Catholic identity. It is no longer so. This change indicates a change in the way most Catholics understand sin as well as their understanding of what it means to be Catholic. It can often indicate a different – and often improved – image of God.

This non-use of confession or of any other form of acknowledgment of sin can create the sense that sin does not matter. Sin does matter. But its importance depends on what is meant by the word. The almost disappearance of the practice of confession in so many parts of the Church may simply mean that many Catholics think that the sins they once confessed do not matter all that much. They may still have a sharp sense of what they really see as sinful. This again underlines the purpose of this book which is to enter into the question of what we mean by 'sin'.

As we shall see, historical studies show us that the practice of confession has been a significant – if not regular – part of Catholic life from the thirteenth century on. The Fourth Lateran Council in 1215 decreed that each Catholic should go to confession at least once a year before Easter. The practice received great emphasis at the Council of Trent and it became a regular part of Catholic life in the nineteenth and earlier twentieth centuries. But it was not part of Catholic life for the first twelve centuries of the Church's existence. What differences are there then between those two long stretches of Catholic history?

A frequent comment regarding sin in recent decades is that people have lost their sense of sin. But it may be that the sense of sin has not so much been lost as that it has changed. As we shall also see further on, the sense of sin has changed along the path of history and it has been shaped by the social and cultural circumstances of the different periods of history. Is a similar re-shaping happening today?

Whatever may be the case with the contemporary sense of sin, there is no lack of a sense of injustice and of the existence of evil in the ethos of contemporary societies, even though what is practically identified as unjust or evil in such societies may vary considerably. Our understanding of sin needs to share ground with the sense of what is wrong, unjust or evil among contemporary people. Believers are part of the society to which they belong and their sense of sin will be influenced by their society. This does not mean that we simply take over our society's perception of 'sin' but it does mean that we speak of sin in dialogue with the world in which we and our contemporaries live. Historically, we will see that this has been the case in the past. As believers, we are not a sect separated from our society but are – and are intended to be – part of the society and culture to which we belong, even though that belonging is given a particular slant by our faith in God's revelation in Christ.[5]

One of the most relevant aspects of the Catholic tradition that needs to be brought to bear in speaking about sin is that we believe in the forgiveness of sin. An overemphasis on sin in preaching, teaching and pastoral practice has given and still can give the wrong balance to the Christian understanding of sin and God's abundant forgiveness. The forgiveness of sin is so central an aspect of Christian faith that it is expressed in both the creeds in common use – the Apostles' Creed and the Nicene Creed. The forgiveness of sin is an article of faith – that is, it is of the core of Christian faith. The thrust of that article of faith ought to give context and shape to our understanding of sin and, so to speak, 'put it in its place'.

A changed sense of sin

One way to correct an inadequate understanding of sin is to tap into the riches of the Scriptures and of the tradition of the faith. As well as delving into the riches of the past to deepen our understanding of sin, we also need – as suggested above – to address the attitudes and questions that contemporary people have about it. Everyone today – believer and nonbeliever alike – is living in a new

---

[5] See especially *Evangelii Gaudium*, no. 115.

and multi-faceted social and cultural context in which the perception of right and wrong has undergone change.

What does the word sin mean to people of our day? There is, of course, no simple answer to that question. But we can pick up some hints that can suggest some shifts in the contemporary mentality in its regard.

Sin and sexuality

One significant hint is that a generation or two ago, there was a strong association between sin and sexuality which is no longer the case. Rightly or wrongly, for younger generations, sin has little to do with sexuality as such. Things that were once considered shameful such as sex before marriage is now the norm for most couples, and is often seen as a lead up to and a testing ground for marriage. Things once considered horrific such as homosexuality are now very differently understood and are largely accepted as part of the woof and weave of human society. It is very different for issues where violence, power or unwanted lust are drawn into sexual activity such as is the case with rape, domestic violence or sexual abuse. In the past such forms of sexual activity were generally kept hidden but now are rightly seen as needing to be dealt with openly and with the aid of the law. Such changes in attitude are significant and exemplify just how much the concept of right and wrong has changed in contemporary society.

Whatever sense of sin there is in contemporary society has expanded well beyond the sphere of sexuality. We need to acknowledge that there has been an over concentration on sexual matters in the course of Christian history; there has been an unsure-footedness in its regard. This is often linked to St Augustine and his rather pessimistic view of human nature that had great historical influence because of Augustine's stature in the development of Western thought both theological and philosophical;[6] and his ideas have had several revivals and re-interpretations in the course of Christian history.

We also need to acknowledge that, from the beginning, the Church has used the human thinking of its time to develop its understanding of morality. Stoicism and Platonism were used in the early centuries of the Church, both of which tended to be negative with regard to sexuality. From the latter half of the twentieth century, more balanced voices have been heard regarding sexuality and marriage.[7]

Sin and the individual

Another hint about the sense of sin today is that, in recent centuries, it tended to be conceived purely in terms of the individual; it concerned only the individual's action or lack of action. As we will see later, this has its origins in the later Middle Ages and increases in importance down into

---

[6] See John Mahoney, *The Making of Moral Theology*. Oxford: Clarendon Press, 1987, pp. 37-71; A. D. Fitzgerald, *Augustine through the Ages. An Encyclopaedia*. Grand rapids, Michigan/Cambridge, UK: William B. Eerdmans Publishing Company, 1999, pp. 800-802 (Entry on Sin).

[7] Quite apart from the work of Catholic theologians, this can be seen in significant recent documents of the Magisterium of which *Amoris Laetitia* of Pope Francis (2016) is a striking example.

the twentieth century. The rising importance given to the individual is a characteristic of the modern era. It came to the fore in the Renaissance[8] (15th century on) and then developed further in the Enlightenment (18th century on). That sense of the value of the individual is a great fruit of modern times. However, as is so often the case, it developed at the expense of other values such as the critical importance of the social dimension of being human.

What is emerging today – as a result of a deeper understanding of the Scriptures, a fuller grasp of the history of the tradition and listening to the signs of the times – is a much broader concept of sin that takes in the individual's action but sees sin as a much deeper and broader reality having communal and structural dimensions within which the individual lives and acts.

Associated with that individualism, in Catholic practice sin was too often reduced to the subjective guilt of the individual person with insufficient regard for the effects emanating from their sinful acts. The making of reparation – which is theologically intrinsic to the sacrament of penance – was often neglected as a result.[9] Having to make reparation to those affected took some account of the social dimension of sin.

---

[8] See Aaron Gurevich, *The Origins of European Individualism*, Oxford/UK & Cambridge USA: Blackwell, 1995; and Peter Burke, *The European Renaissance*: Oxford: Blackwell Publishers, 1998, 217-225.

[9] John Mahoney, *op. cit.*, pp. 175-222.

World-wide awareness

Another significant change in the last century is that, thanks to the influence of a worldwide media, people no longer live within their own immediate societies as was so much the case before the twentieth century. Now people have access to what is happening throughout the world. Such broadening of awareness has created a greater understanding of the evils that can and do bedevil our world. In the light of this awareness, a purely individualist approach to sin can seem trivial.

The human sciences

The psychological sciences have also shifted the general sense of wrongdoing or sin. Many of the offences that were considered sinful in the past are now seen as arising from illnesses or wounds of the person's psyche that call for healing rather than for forgiveness. The psychological sciences must have their voice in the question of sinfulness and human frailty; and they are now taken into account in theology and in official Church teaching.[10] The insights arising from these sciences are a stimulus to seeing human actions more realistically and at greater depth. They stimulate new insights into the reality of human sinfulness, that they by no means deny.

The sociological sciences also have their place in helping to understand the dynamics of human societies and of the individuals living within them. Understanding these

---

[10] *Evangelii Gaudium*, no. 40.

dynamics helps us to understand the powerful social forces at work in all human beings and so helps us to understand the social dimension of human sinfulness.

Secular society

In the contemporary context, there is also a need to be careful in the use of the word 'sin'. Sin, as we shall see, is a word that in principle belongs within the context of belief in God. It embodies a particular insight into human wrongdoing that arises out of faith in God because it sees wrongdoing as detrimental to relationship with God.

In our secular social setting, the word 'sin' can be seen as unreal or even a source of amusement to those who do not share the Christian tradition. To make the gospel significant in a society such as our own, it is important that our terminology has traction with contemporary people, including contemporary believers. What is called sin within the Christian tradition may refer to things that contemporary society might call by other names such as injustice, crime, evil or simply wrongdoing.

In speaking of the secular nature of our society, a radical question faces any such society and that is 'where does it find its moral criteria?' Every society has to have such a point of reference. Without such a point of reference, does such a society only have recourse to identifying morality with law for lack of other options? Or is recourse taken to such simplistic criteria as something being named as 'un-Australian'? We hear such a term used frequently in the political sphere and in the media. Is use of such a term even prone to xenophobia?

This raises the question of a need for objective criteria of morality that go beyond the feelings or even the convictions of individuals to ensure the wellbeing of the whole of society and so of the individuals within it. This is an area that calls for the resources of the biblical and Christian traditions to be at the service of the whole of society. It is a service that can only be rendered in a genuine other-centred dialogue with our contemporary secular societies. And it is worth remembering that these societies still have within them something of the leaven of their Christian past.

The gospel and sin

The word sin is ingrained in the Christian tradition: it is irreversibly present in the Scriptures, in the writings of the tradition and in contemporary theological and pastoral thought. It comes up frequently in the celebration of Mass: we hear the word 'sin' in the readings and prayers, in the Gloria, in the Creed and in the Eucharistic Prayers, in the words of the Lord over the cup that end with the phrase 'for the forgiveness of sins', at the Breaking of the Bread where we hail Christ as 'The Lamb of God who takes away the sins of the world' and again at the Invitation to Communion where we hear: 'Behold the Lamb of God, behold him who takes away the sins of the world'.

What does the contemporary community gathered for Mass make of the word 'sin' or 'sins' in those significant parts of the Mass? Do they see it as referring to real offences and/or the peccadillos of each person there? Or does it refer to a larger reality than these? Or does it perhaps indicate that are we too concerned about sin?

There may be problems with the perceived meaning of the word 'sin' but its constant use in understanding the role of Christ as Saviour means that it is a word that has profound significance for the understanding of faith in Christ. It is integral to the proclamation of the gospel.

Sin: a serious issue

Sin is a serious matter. At this point, let us describe sin as human involvement in wrongdoing or evil. This is a tentative description that provides us with a starting point to continue our discussion.

Human involvement with wrongdoing or evil is an all too apparent aspect of human existence and history; it is a force to be reckoned with. By comparison to the evil done throughout the world of which we are now so much more conscious, the way sin has been commonly spoken about in the Church in recent centuries can seem too narrow and individualistic and even, perhaps, irrelevant.

Those of us of generations that stretch back beyond the 1960s will remember being told about mortal sin, venial sin and original sin. Mortal sin involved significant violations of the ten commandments or other enshrined standards, or by committing such 'Catholic' offences as missing Mass on Sunday, eating meat on Friday or getting married outside the Church. These sins were put on the same level of seriousness as had been murder, adultery and idolatry in the first centuries of the Church. Such 'mortal' sins excluded the perpetrator from receiving communion and thus from the heart of the life of the Church. Mortal sin was seen as threatening the offender with hell.

Venial sin concerned smaller instances of sinfulness. They did not exclude the person from the life of the Church or break the person's relationship with God , but were seen as weakening that relationship.[11]

Original sin was identified with a literal understanding of the sin of Adam and Eve as recounted in chapters two and three of the book of Genesis along with their handing on of that sinfulness to all their descendants.

As the knowledge of the Scriptures and the tradition increased throughout the twentieth century, the treatment of the story of Adam and Eve as an historical narrative was seen to be misplaced. Along with that, the then current approach to sin in general was gradually coming under review.

There was a certain ambiguity in the practice and mentality of recent centuries, which was – at least partly – the result of different theological schools of thought. On the one hand, the subjective side of sin was predominant that is, the penitent's intention and their degree of responsibility; on the other hand, sin could be over-identified with the external acts of sin to the neglect of its subjective, interior side. As a result of this latter approach, there was a tendency to confess such external acts as missing Mass on Sunday

---

[11] *Catechism for General Use in Australia*. Melbourne: Australian Catholic Truth Society, 1938. See p. 23, questions 93-97.

even in circumstances where it was physically impossible to do so.

In catechesis, criteria were set forth to assess what sins were mortal; hence, the three criteria of serious matter, full knowledge and full consent. The last two of these were not always easy for people to assess and were not seen as being as important as the seriousness of the matter. Significantly, in sexual matters, there was no venial sin (technically referred to as there being no 'parvity' of matter in sexual sins). All sexual sin was considered serious sin!

Another crucial element in the understanding of sin was that the mentality and practice of the time was cast in a legal framework.[12] The catechism in use in Australia in the first half of the twentieth century described sin as 'any thought, word, deed or omission against the law of God'[13] This clearly put the understanding of sin in the particular category of law.

In the general thinking of the Church about sin up to the middle decades of the twentieth century, there was little genuine reference to the biblical tradition with its much deeper and more realistic understanding of human sinfulness. The problem with the legal approach was not so much that it was legalistic, but simply that it was legal. Sin was understood in legal categories and within a legal mindset. This approach to sin carried with it at least an implied image of God as the law maker to whom

---

[12] For a deeper presentation of the influence of law, see John Mahoney, *op. cit.*, chapter 4: The Language of Law (pp. 224-258).

[13] *Catechism for General Use in Australia*. Melbourne: Australian Catholic Truth Society, 1938, p. 21, Question 82.

obedience was owed and who would deal out appropriate punishment. The Council of Trent explicitly saw the role of the priest in the confessional in legal terms, speaking of him as acting as a judge.[14]

There are some historical reasons behind this recourse to the legal. Following the Council of Trent, there was great need for reform in the Catholic Church and there was an urgency in Catholic circles to make sure that the moral corruption of the Late Middle Ages was never repeated. This concern was always in the background in the disputes between Catholic reformers and Protestant theologians. A legal approach fitted the bill for these reformers. At the time, there was also a renewed emphasis on authority in the Church, especially that of the Papacy. And at hand there was the obvious model of the ten commandments and later the commandments of the Church to fall back on as a charter for reform. Catholic parish missions were a primary feature of the efforts towards reform and they laid great emphasis on moral reform, sin, purgatory, hell and the need to go to confession. Such missions varied in sophistication, dramatic presentation and doctrinal refinement.

We cannot continue to speak of sin and forgiveness in the same terms as we did in the past and expect to be well understood and received. Rethinking our understanding of sin is one of the changes needed if we are to be able to

---

[14] 'tamquam a iudice' Council of Trent, Session XIV, chapter 6. Denzinger & Schonmetzer, *Enchiridion Symbolorum, Definitionum et Declarationum de rebus fidei et morum.* Barcelona, Freiburg in Beisgau, Rome, NY: Herder, 1965, no. 1685.

make the gospel heard in our society today. It is a necessary element of evangelisation.

As Christians, we are committed to speaking about sin as part of the history and existence of the human race which Christ has redeemed; but such speaking needs to touch the reality that people are living today. The effective proclamation of the gospel requires change. As Pope Francis puts it: 'Whenever we make the effort to return to the source and to recover the original freshness of the gospel, new avenues arise, new paths of creativity open up, with different forms of expression, more eloquent signs and words with new meaning for today's world. Every form of authentic evangelisation is always "new"'.[15] The incarnating of the gospel involves a commitment to a dialogue with each culture in which the Christian community exists and to listening to the signs of the times as human history moves on.

Into the future

The situation we are living through today is one in which there is a diversity of mentalities and so it requires honest dialogue. This contrast of mentalities is characteristic of the life of the Church in the new pluralistic and secular societies of the Western world. It is this situation which Vatican II's document on the Church in the Contemporary World began to deal with. This diversity involves the fact that human beings are thinking differently about themselves than they

---

[15] *Evangelii Gaudium*, 11.

did in the past. And this, of course, influences the moral dimension of human and Christian life and so is a crucial factor in presenting an understanding of sin. I want to quote two moral theologians who outline the contrasting attitudes at work in the area of the understanding of human sinfulness.

The first of these theologians is Francine Charoy, a French moral theologian, who in the following quotation outlines the differences of mentality that confront us today as we attempt to speak about sin or any area of morality. She writes:

> For a long time, sin has been the central category of a legally oriented moral theology, which was based on what was permitted and what was forbidden. Also its connection with the fundamentals of theology had been lost.
>
> In the minds of our contemporaries, such an understanding of morality has the feel of a judgment that is grounded in a tradition built on a non-historical prescriptive body of knowledge that denies the value of the singularity of the person and of the particularity of specific historical circumstances. It is often associated with a blame-oriented moralism seen as linked to a clerical power that is itself contested in their minds. It is seen as based on a theological anthropology that presupposes a human consciousness that is transparent to itself.
>
> In the same contemporary minds, such a morality is associated with an external pre-established judgment that uses the fear of damnation as a motive and is imbued with legalism. In other words, such a contemporary mentality is opposed to all moral authority that does not recognise

the capacity of free and autonomous subjects to discern and act out moral judgments in their concrete lives.[16]

Charoy goes on to say 'For many, sin has lost its power to interpret human life and the practice of the confession of sins has lost its power for reconciliation'.[17]

Many issues are raised in this quotation that need further development. It gives expression to significant characteristics of contemporary mindsets that need to be taken into account in order to speak effectively about sin today.

Apart from its clear statement about the problem of understanding morality in legal categories, it makes clear the need to consider not just universal principles but particular concrete people and circumstances. Similarly, it makes clear the expectation of people today to have their capacity for moral discernment recognised and honoured.

The statement that moral theology had lost its connection to the fundamentals of theology is making the point that, in the past, it did not take its inspiration from the Scriptures or from an understanding of the fundamental revelation of God in the Mystery of Christ.

The same quotation also points out that human conscious-ness is not always 'transparent to itself'. This is a most important point for contemporary moral thinking. There are reasons behind human attitudes and actions that are not

---

[16] Francine Charoy, 'Est-il pertinent de rehabiliter le concept de peche en theologie morale catholique?' in Institut Superior des etudes oecumeniques, *Comment parler du peche aujourd'hui?* Paris: Les Editions du Cerf, 2020, 128-9. (Author's translation).

[17] Ibid. 129.

necessarily apparent to our own selves or to other people. This brings in the need to understand the complexity of the human psyche and the need to use the psychological sciences to understand more deeply and accurately human attitudes and action and the sinfulness that can occur as part of them.

Charoy also puts her finger on the point that 'sin has lost its power to help us interpret human life and the confession of sins had lost its power for reconciliation'. This statement is important because sin is part of the Christian interpretation of life and as such needs to be presented effectively. And in stating that the confession of sins has lost its power for reconciliation, she highlights the reality that Christians are no longer finding the traditional form of the sacrament of penance satisfactory.

The other theologian I would like to quote is the moral theologian James Keenan. He suggests that 'we are on the verge of seeing a newer, more robust and definitely more social understanding of sin emerging that... seems more interested in the fact and pervasiveness of sin as well as its roots in the human condition and our social structures'.[18]

Charoy offers us a critique of what we have received and Keenan sets our sights on the future.

An understanding of human sinfulness along the lines suggested by Keenan sets a new path for the understanding of sin, conversion and forgiveness as it does for our

---

[18] James Keenan, 'Raising Expectations on Sin', in *Theological Studies* 77,1 (2015), 165.

celebrations of God's forgiveness in the various rites of penance and reconciliation.

Believing in the forgiveness of sins

In the Apostles' Creed, we profess that we believe in the forgiveness of sins; and in the Nicene Creed 'we confess one Baptism for the forgiveness of sins'. In both cases, this article of faith is placed within the third part of the Creed that expresses Christian faith in the Holy Spirit, one of whose gifts is the forgiveness of sin.

God's forgiveness and the role of the Holy Spirit in that forgiveness is also expressed in the formula of absolution in the sacrament of penance: 'God, the Father of mercies, through the death and resurrection of his Son has reconciled the world to himself and has sent the Holy Spirit among us for the forgiveness of sins; through the ministry of the Church may God give you pardon and peace, and I absolve you from all your sins in the name of the Father, and of the Son, and of the Holy Spirit'. Notice that the last phrase of that formula echoes and applies to the penitent its first phrase in which the activity of Father, Son and Holy Spirit are proclaimed. It is this reconciling action of Father, Son and Spirit that is being brought into the life of the penitent.

We can apply to this sacramental reconciliation the following words of St Paul: 'So for anyone who is in Christ, there is a new creation; the old order is gone and a new being is there to see. It is all God's work; he reconciled us to himself through Christ and gave us the ministry of reconciliation. I mean, God was in Christ reconciling the world to himself, not holding anyone's faults against them, but entrusting to us the message of reconciliation' (2 Corinthians 5:17-19).

The capital point in all of this is that we believe in the forgiveness of sin not just as a juridical declaration of forgiveness, but as the power of Christ's death and resurrection being applied to us. That death and resurrection that overcomes sin and draws us into union with the Father. We believe in the constant radical action of the Holy Spirit who never ceases to be at work, seeking to draw us out of sinfulness into union with the Son and the Father. Therefore, we do not believe that sin has the last word, we do not believe that it has the ultimate power to define human beings.

Belief in the forgiveness of sin arises, of course, from faith in God as God is revealed by Jesus. As already mentioned, sin is revealed specifically as sin – rather than as just wrongdoing or injustice – in the relationship with God that is revealed in the biblical tradition. It is in the forgiveness of God that sin – that the Scriptures see as separation from God – is overcome by the loving goodness of God, who draws us into union with himself. The sacrament brings the presence and activity of God to bear in the healing of the separation that sin creates.

Returning to the creeds, there is something of a difference between the formulations given in the two creeds. The Apostles' Creed speaks generically about forgiveness and the Nicene Creed specifies forgiveness associated with baptism. This belief in God's forgiveness of sin is the ground out of which there arises a specific sacrament for the forgiveness of sins committed after baptism. In the first centuries of Christianity, there emerged a rite of penance for those who had sinned seriously after baptism. It was designed only for very serious sin.

There was opposition among early Christians to such a rite. In the opinion of those who opposed the rite, such sinners were to be left to 'the mercy of God'. These people held to the belief that baptism was the only means for the forgiveness of sin. The emergence of another rite for the forgiveness of sin was a point of strong contention especially in the aftermath of persecutions during which some Christians denied their faith or took measures to save themselves from arrest by means such as the bribery of Roman officials. Could such Christians be readmitted to the Church? Was sin forgivable after baptism? Eventually, it was resolved that such Christians could be readmitted to the Church but only after a demanding process of re-conversion that will be discussed in more detail in the next chapter.

Belief in the forgiveness of sin is a critical element in the presentation of the gospel today. Is there not a tendency in our contemporary societies to see sin as more powerful than goodness and forgiveness? Once someone has sinned seriously, do they not become identified with their sin? Is there a distinction between the sin and the sinner? There tends to be no exit for some sinners from their sin.

This corresponds to the attitude of some in the early Church who thought that there could be no forgiveness after baptism. They thought that those who promoted forgiveness were too lenient. Such attitudes are reminiscent of those people in the Gospels who thought that Jesus was erring when he mixed with, ate with and forgave sinners.

Does such an attitude underlie contemporary issues such as the purpose of imprisonment? Is it purely for containment of those to whom there is nothing more than their 'sin' or does it involve the possibility of rehabilitation? Does it apply to public figures who may have done serious wrong, but is there no exit for them? Are they definitively to be identified with their wrongdoing? The same question can also be asked about sexual offenders.

No human being and no society can afford to ignore the words of Jesus in John's Gospel: 'Let the one without sin cast the first stone' (John 8:7). In terms of the Gospel, the only closed door to exiting out of sinfulness is the one that the offenders themselves have locked.

Sin and goodness

Before moving on, I would like to make the following point. This book is about the understanding of sin; consequently, that is what it will be dealing with for the most part. But this sinfulness needs to be seen alongside the goodness of human beings that is so much a part of everyday human experience. The sinfulness that is found in humankind is only one dimension of humanity and should not be presented without sufficient recognition of human goodness.

Exaggerated presentations of sin fly in the face of the common experience of people. The goodness that is so really a part of human beings must not be left in shadow. As we will see later on, God created human beings and saw them as very good and God continues creating us and seeing the goodness in us. The second account of creation speaks of God breathing the breath of life into those symbolic figures, Adam and Eve. And as we shall also see, the two of them represent all of us into whom God continues to breathe the breath of life. What the faithful God begins, he continues and brings to its fulfilment.

There is an ambiguity in human beings between their goodness and their sinfulness. This ambiguity often comes out in the moments of crisis or pressure. Such 'times' are described by a different word in the Scriptures to the word used for the ordinary run of time. The word for ordinary time in Greek is *chronos* – from which we get such words as chronology – which just means the flow of time. But the critical times are referred to by the word *kairos* – they are the times of crisis, the times of testing.

We pray in the Lord's prayer 'Lead us not into temptation' which would be better translated 'Do not put us to the test'. This phrase is a reference to the crisis times. The balance of goodness and sinfulness in human beings is often manifested in the testing or crisis moments. Such times may be those when we are subject to threat or fear, or when we are faced with a necessary and crucial life-defining choice. Such instances occur in all human lives. The prayer 'Do not put us to the test' is a prayer rooted in the self-knowledge that we can indeed to tempted to take a wrong or false path or to close off from the future offered us. And these are also times when we need to call upon the Father in heaven to deliver us from evil.

A postscript: an example of development

The development of the 'sacrament 'of penance, whose first step is described above, is a good example of the way development comes about in the Church. The principle of forgiveness is clearly presented in the Gospels and is central to the meaning of the death and resurrection of Jesus. But how was this forgiveness to be worked out in unforeseen circumstances? If baptism put an end to sin, what is to be done about serious sin occurring after baptism? What did forgiveness apply to and what did it not apply to?

To the question of serious sin after baptism, there seemed to be no clear and obvious answer; the resolution of the issue had to be worked out. As we have seen there were differences of opinion about whether there should be such a rite at all. Those favouring the use of such a rite found the model for that rite in the process leading up to baptism since baptism was 'for the forgiveness of sins'.

As circumstances changed and the life and thinking of the Church developed, there also developed a deeper appreciation of the depth and constancy of God's forgiveness.

We also see in this development the fact that Christianity is truly historical. It is subject to the events and unexpected changes and circumstances that factually occur in the course of actual human existence. Everything had not been prepared and set down beforehand.

Chapter 2

A History of Change and Continuity

I n taking up an historical perspective on any area of the Church's life, we need to be aware of the influence of the culture of each time on the way in which the Church interprets and hands on its received tradition. The context in which the faith is lived out has an intrinsic influence on how the faith is understood and passed on. This applies to past periods of the Church's life as it applies to the present time.[19]

Regarding the history of the Christian tradition on sin, there is much scholarly work yet to be done in tracing the history of its understanding in the various historical periods

---

[19] There is no way to peel the culture of the time off the tradition. The tradition is always lived within a culture. This has been so from the very beginning of Christianity. The original revelation in Jesus and the initial handing on of that revelation took place within the Jewish culture of Jesus' and the apostles' time. Within the New Testament writings, we can already see a transition taking place into the culture of the world beyond Judaism. The Christian tradition has then been handed on in and through many other cultures in the course of the last two millennia. So we are always dealing with a continuity of faith in differing cultural forms. And the influence of the culture of the time has to be taken into account in order for the gospel to be communicable while at the same time the culture has to be critically discerned so that it does not distort the tradition. This is a major part of the theologian's task.

of the Church's life. There are hints regarding this history in a few works that look particularly at the sins that were the paradigmatic or mentality-shaping sins of their period – the sins that revealed something of the mentality of the time.[20] These hints, however, only give us small cameos; there is a much wider history that has yet to be filled in.

In the last chapter, we saw something of the beginnings of the development of a rite of the forgiveness of sins for those Christians who sinned seriously after baptism. In the course of the many centuries to follow, there would be considerable changes to the way in which this forgiveness was understood and ritualised. And in each of these major developments, we can discern differences in the understanding of sin. These differing concepts reflected the culture and historical circumstances of the times in which those believers lived.

---

[20] Louis-Marie Chauvet, Pratiques penitentielles et conceptions du péché. *Le Supplément* 120-121 (1977) 41-64; John Bossy, *Christianity in the West 1400-1700*, Oxford/NY : OUP, 1998, 35-56 ; M. F. Berrouard, *La pénitence publique durant les six premiers siècles : histoire et sociologie*. Maison-Dieu 118 (1974), 92-130; John Mahoney, *The Making of Moral Theology. A Study of the Roman Catholic Tradition*. Oxford: Clarendon Press, 1987; Paula Fredrik Sen, *The Early History of an Idea*. Princeton and Oxford: Princeton University Press, 2012; Kyle Harper, *From Shame to Sin. The Christian Transformation of Sexual Morality in Late Antiquity*, Cambridge, Massachusetts/London, England: Harvard University Press, 2013; John Portman, *History of Sin. Its Evolution to Today and Beyond*, London, Boulder, NY, Toronto, Plymouth UK: Roman & Littlefield Publishers Inc., 2007.

The various forms that the rite of penance[21] has taken over the centuries give us some insight into historical differences in the conception of sin in those different periods of the Church's history.[22] These rites were formed in response to sin as it was experienced and perceived in each of those times. In these instances, we are not dealing so much with an organised theology of sin but rather with a perception of sin based on experience and formed in dialogue with the scriptural word of God.

Sin and the first form of penance

The initial form of the rite penance (2nd-5th centuries) excluded the serious sinner from the life of the Church. It was used only for those sins considered to be very serious at the time: idolatry, adultery and murder. Other sins were dealt simply by participating in the life and prayer of the Church. Those three serious sins were seen as contradicting the person's very belonging to the Christian community.

As mentioned earlier, the penitents came back into the life of the Church by means of a virtual repetition of the process of initiation by which they had originally become Christians. This process put the penitents into a

---

[21] I am using the phrase 'rite of penance' rather than 'sacrament' of penance because penance was not spoken of as a sacrament alongside the major sacraments of Baptism and the Eucharist until the 12th/13th century when it was listed among the seven sacraments. Previous to that, it was part of the wide network of rites of the Church that were considered 'sacramenta' in a broader sense to that which we are accustomed to understand today.

[22] For a somewhat fuller treatment of these cameos, see Frank O'Loughlin, *The Future of the Sacrament of Penance*. Strathfield, NSW: St Pauls, 2007, 11-87.

particular group within the Church, called the order of penitents, just as they had belonged to another group, the order of catechumens, during their preparation for baptism. The process of their re-admission to the Eucharist and so to the life of the Church was modelled on the process they had been through leading up to their baptism. The establishment of this process gives a strong sense of just how seriously those three sins were taken.

As a consequence of these two processes being virtually the same, it was thought that since baptism could be received only once, so also penance could be received only once. Characteristic of this form of penance was that it involved not just the penitent or the bishop but the whole community of the Church. It was an explicitly ecclesial process, just as was the order of catechumens.

However, this first form of penance proved unworkable as the Church emerged from its initial historical form of rather intense small communities and moved into a new historical situation in which it gradually came to include the whole population of the Roman Empire. This change occurred from the fourth and fifth centuries on. The first form of penance was effective within those earlier relatively small communities but was quite impractical in the new situation into which the Church was entering.

Despite the insistence of many Church leaders that the earlier form of penance was the only form that could be legitimately used, it proved impossibly demanding for these later differently initiated Christians and so gradually it fell into disuse. Penance disappeared from the lives of most believers; it came to be used as people came close to death. New historical circumstances changed things radically as the Church became the Church of a large population. This affected virtually every aspect of the life of the Church. As part of this change, the process of initiation changed: the catechumenate gradually died out and infant baptism became the common form of baptism. The rite of penance – originally based on baptism – lost that link to baptism and followed a more penitential path that we shall describe as its history unfolds.

The concept of sin at work in that first form of penance was centred on the three sins considered as placing the sinner outside the Christian community: idolatry, murder and adultery. Idolatry was especially serious because worshipping other gods betrayed the very core of Christianity. And it remained a dangerous possibility for Christians who were at least under the threat of possible persecution in which they could be required to offer incense to the gods of Rome and to the emperor. Murder, of course, offended against the sacredness of life and adultery was a touchstone of Christian identity in a world where the relationship of marriage was not in principle highly regarded.

As time went on, a wider range of sins became subject to this discipline at least in those places where it actually continued to be used.

Sin and the second form of penance

The first form of penance was succeeded in a rather piecemeal and often disputed fashion by a form of penance brought to the continent of Europe by Irish missionary monks. Its origin was in the Irish monasteries that were at the core of the well-developed Irish Christian culture. Transported to Europe, this form of penance was used among the unsettled and volatile population of the continent as it was at that time. It began to be used there from the later decades of the sixth century. This form of penance was based on books called Penitentials that listed the appropriate penances for a wide range of offences. To each offence there was a penance, and to multiple offences, a multiplication of penances. For this reason, it is often called Tariff penance. This form of penance involved a personal confession of sins and the receiving of a heavy penance to be performed. There was no formal giving of absolution. In contrast to the previous form, it could be used as many times as the penitent wished.

This form of penance was used in a Europe made up mainly of tribal societies whose sense of solidarity among their members and particularly with their leader was such that they could do each other's penances! Such a sharing of penance may make little sense to our contemporary way of thinking but it reflects one of those historical conditionings that seem strange to later generations but were not so in their own time. It implied a different understanding of human life, human community and human sin which those peoples took for granted. It involved a strong predominance of the communal or tribal dimension of society over that of the individual member.

Behind the use of this second historical form of penance, there lay a different sense of sin. It was influenced by the taboo mentality of those European peoples. This meant that

41

even an unintended offence had to have reparation made for it to save the perpetrator from its consequences. Underneath that demand for reparation lurked a strong belief in the power of fate. Such a belief in fate minimised the role of human freedom and it did not accept that sin could simply be forgiven. Along with the belief in fate, the mentality of the time fell back on a morality based on principles that were the equivalent of that expressed in the Old Testament phrase: 'an eye for an eye and a tooth for a tooth'. And so the revenge of those offended was an accepted yet disturbing factor in the functioning of those societies.

The penitential books worked within that mentality but also laid the grounds for surpassing it by their emphasis on the intention of the offender and on sins committed in mind and heart. So the balance between human freedom and the perceived power of fate began to shift. By this means, a more personal notion of sin was being promoted and the possibility of forgiveness was being made concrete. Much of the use of this form continued to be centred on monks, especially those of the Irish tradition. Monks and monasteries were at that time in Europe's history a strong force for social and cultural change.

Sin and the third form of penance

In the twelfth and thirteenth centuries, a new rite of penance was emerging. In keeping with cultural changes that were giving more importance to the individual, an individual and confidential rite of penance was gradually taking form. In this rite an individual penitent confessed their sins to a priest in private with a view to receiving absolution from those sins. This practice possibly had some roots in the ancient practice of spiritual direction. It is this form of penance – with some modifications – that has been handed down into the twentieth and twenty-first centuries.

In the period preceding the Council of Trent and in the centuries following it, this form of penance was thought to be the only form that the sacrament had ever taken. An insufficient knowledge of earlier history and the need to defend Catholic practices against the Protestant reforming ideas led to the earlier forms of penance falling out of the Church's awareness.

This new practice shifted the understanding of sin into an individualist mode. Over its history, this new rite was used in a variety of ways: its earlier forms required a good deal more ritual and prayer than later ones. As time went on, all that remained was a bare minimum of ritual.[23] In the course of several centuries, this tendency to minimise what was required to happen in the rite was in part due to the increased number of people 'going to confession'. One element in the ritual that was greatly increased was the requirement that the penitent tell all their sins. The telling of sins expanded into the telling of all one's sins in kind and number, and this applied to even very minor sins. There was also increasing encouragement to confess one's sins frequently.

The concept of sin implied in this form of penance varies somewhat in accord with the varieties of its use. What did

---

[23] See Frank O'Loughlin, *op. cit.*, pp. 65-6.

stand out in all of its uses and what increased with the passing of time was that sin was conceived purely as the act of an individual. This became so much the case that when the question of social and structural sin arose in the twentieth century, many thought that such things could not be called sin precisely because the word sin was so strongly identified with the acts of an individual person.

Implied in this very individualistic practice was the limitation of the meaning of sin to sins. There was a strong concentration on sinful acts as distinct from one's sinfulness and from the ongoing influence of sin within and around us. So in confession one could be rid of all one's sins and be 'clean' again – at least until there were more sins to be confessed and so 'cleansed' from.

In looking at these different forms of penance, we can see that there have been very considerable changes in the practices of penance over the long term. There was the change from penance being possible only once in a lifetime to being very frequent; from being for only very major sins to all sins; from being a long process involving years to a matter of minutes; from being a communal act of the Church to involving only the individual; from involving many rites to a minimum of rites. In each of these there was a differing conception of sin involved. Each of these forms were tied into particular historical circumstances and different cultures.

Today as we live in a period of great cultural change would we not expect that this change would influence the understanding of sin and the use of rites of penance?

Further Historical Perspectives on Sin

The 'Catholic' sins

Apart from the concept of sin involved in the historical rites of penance, there are other identifiable conceptions of sin at work in the history of Catholicism. In the post-Reformation period, there was an emphasis on sins that earlier on we called the 'Catholic' sins. These were such things missing Mass on Sunday, eating meat on Friday or marrying outside the Church. These were considered grave sins – mortal sins impeding the person's going to communion. They were, in the Catholic culture of their time, the equivalent of idolatry, adultery, murder in the earliest form of penance that also excluded those who committed such sins from receiving communion. We have in these 'Catholic' sins a good example of the historical conditioning of the way that sin has been conceived.

These 'Catholic' sins took their importance from the state of conflict between the Catholic Church and the Churches arising from the Reformation. This conflict was a dominant dimension of the life of the Church in the whole of the Post-Reformation period. These sins were seen as involving Catholic identity and keeping yourself on the right side of the line separating Catholics from Protestants. In some circumstances, the deliberate neglect of these practices was indeed a sign of the person's separating themselves from the Catholic Church. The perceived seriousness of these sins has disappeared because the situation that gave them their seriousness has disappeared.

Interdicts and excommunications

Another practice that appears in the history of the Church and had its effects on the conception of sin is that of popes or bishops declaring some practice or other a mortal sin or of imposing excommunication on individuals or sometimes on whole regions of Europe. Such practices arise from a conception of the Church that exaggerated the power of the keys spoken of in Matthew 16:13-20. Such usages tended to remove the necessary distance between Christ and the hierarchy of the Church. They belonged to a time when Church authorities had sometimes direct and sometimes indirect but effective civil power. Such practices had a deleterious influence on the general sense of sin, especially when they were used with political motivations.

Legalism

Yet another element shaping the conception of sin throughout most of the period following the Reformation and the Council of Trent was the already discussed influence of a legal mentality. Law is a necessity for all human societies – including the Church – but law needs to remain in its own sphere and not absorb other dimensions of life. Law is not theology though, hopefully, the two are in dialogue.

Law is not spirituality but hopefully it is aware of such deeper dimensions of Christian life. In a period whose mentality tended to be overly legal, the law encroached on theology and could take over from spirituality. At times, Catholic spirituality seemed to be reduced to obedience to the Church's law.[24]

Sin and sexuality

The early seventeenth century saw another significant social development that had an influence on the conception of sin and especially on the frequent identification of sin and sexuality. A change came over European culture around that time that reshaped the cultural attitude to sexuality.

Before this time, sexual explicitness was an unashamed part of normally accepted discourse. Such talk has always been part of human discourse; what became different in this period is that there came to be a touch of shame or at least embarrassment about such talk. Consequently, it would tend to cease when women or children or perhaps even the clergy entered the scene. It is suggested that that would not have been the case in earlier bawdier times, because of their more open attitude to sexuality that was neither hidden nor a cause for embarrassment. Sexual references were part of the openly accepted run of life. Such references were even an unembarrassed part of the discourse of preachers.

---

[24] There is a deeper discussion of this problem especially regarding the balance of obedience and personal initiative in Yves Congar, *The Word and the Spirit*. London: Geoffrey Chapman/San Francisco: Harper and Row Publishers, 1986, pp. 53-55.

From the early seventeenth century on, a new attitude to sexuality arises in which it becomes a very private, even a secret thing; it was not talked about in respectable company and was not even publicly acknowledged. Historians note that it was around this time that houses began to be built differently: they were built in such a way that there was a bedroom for husband and wife, a bedroom for the boys and one for the girls. This was especially so in the ascendant middle class of the time.[25]

The suggestion is that this brought about a hiddenness and secrecy regarding sexuality and that, as a consequence, sexuality became more mysterious and intriguing. On the other hand, this changed attitude had the very positive effect of emphasising the personal character of the marriage relationship.

The new form of home architecture arising in this period was in contrast to the Medieval situation in which common sleeping quarters were usual for the greater part of the population. This was so even in the courts of the aristocracy, with the exception perhaps of the Lord and Lady's chamber. This form of sleeping quarters continued for the poorer sections of most of the population whose dwellings consisted of one room. This situation has

---

[25] John Bossy, *Christianity in the West 1400-1700*, Oxford/NY: OUP. 1985, pp. 33-35; M. Foucault, *The History of Sexuality*, Vol.1. NY: Vintage Books (Random House),1978,1-13; Roger Chartier (ed.), *A History of Private Life. Vol. III: Passions of the Renaissance*. Cambridge/Massachusetts & London/England: The Belknap Press of Harvard University Press, 1989, pp. 493-529, esp. pp. 507-9.

prevailed among poorer people down in to the twentieth and twenty-first centuries.

Jansenism

Another phenomenon of the seventeenth century that affected the sense of sin was Jansenism.[26] It is named after a Louvain theologian, Cornelius Jansen, who died in 1638. The difference between Jansen and Jansenism is the subject of debate. The movement that claimed him as their inspiration was an attempt at tightening morality in the Church; it was an attempt that went to extremes.

At its core, Jansenism had a very pessimistic view of human nature, seeing it as pervaded by sin; it considered even slight sins as impediments to the receiving of communion. It promoted infrequent communion because of its belief in the persistent sinfulness of human beings. It had long-term influence on the Church generally but especially on the Church in France and areas influenced by it. Jansenism was condemned by Roman authorities in 1653 but it long continued to have considerable influence on the everyday life of the Church.

One of the aims of Pope Pius X's decrees on frequent communion and on earlier communion for children was to overcome remaining Jansenistic views about the receiving of communion. Jansenism's emphasis on sin made sin seem more powerful than God's forgiveness and distorted the Christian tradition. The mercy of God was clouded

---

[26] John Mahoney, *op. cit.*, pp. 89-96, 139-143.

by Jansenism's self-righteous and extreme perfectionism. Underlying it there is an image of God that does not gel with 'the Father of our Lord Jesus Christ' presented in the new testament.

These cameos of sin in the history of the Church illustrate something of the history of the understanding of sin, that has varied in the Church's practice and theology. In our context today, we need to re-examine the understanding of sin by tapping into the Scriptures and the tradition and then working toward an understanding of sin that takes into account the pluralist and secular context of the twenty-first century.

Chapter 3

Sin, a Human Reality, Biblical Discovery

Human sinfulness has been brought into the light in a unique way in the biblical tradition. In the course of the long history represented by the Old and New Testaments, the deepest reality of sin has been identified as dissociation and separation from God. For the Scriptures, this state of separation from God has the effect of creating a distortion in human beings and between human beings.

As we look into what the Scriptures mean by sin, we need to be ready to let ourselves think differently about it. The Scriptures lead us to see a deep and complex reality when they speak of sin.

The biblical tradition has its origins in a relationship between God and human beings that it calls the covenant. The word covenant means an agreement or a pact or an alliance; it describes an ongoing established relationship. The biblical covenant came about on the initiative of God and the most outstanding thing to emerge from it was the revelation of God as personal, as one with whom human beings can have a relationship.

In this covenant that began to come about with Abraham (Genesis 12:1-9), human beings were called into a new discovery of God. In this discovery, God emerges not as a force in the universe or one of a panoply of gods but as the one and only God who relates personally to human beings and mysteriously interacts with them. The principal image used to describe this covenant is that of marriage:[27] God imaged himself as the spouse of Israel. In the New Testament, this image was extended to the relationship of Christ and his people.[28]

God is personal and the response – or lack thereof – of his covenant partner matters. Sin emerges as an offence against this relationship between God and his people. The paradigm of sin is therefore idolatry that is described in terms of adultery – Israel running off after other gods. In this way, sin is revealed in its deepest dimension – a breaking-up with God.

This covenant concerns all of humankind. It is mediated by the People of God in both the covenant with Israel and the Christian covenant. They are chosen to be its tangible embodiment in the midst of humanity, but the ultimate purpose of the covenant is to bring all human beings into relationship with God. Abraham, the father of the covenant peoples, is to be a blessing for all of humankind (Genesis 12:2-3).

The personal nature of this revelation of God is fundamental throughout the Scriptures and finds expression in such a

---

[27] See Deuteronomy 7:7-11; Isaiah 54:5-9; 62.3-5; Jeremiah 31:3-4; Ezekiel 16; Hosea 1 and 2.
[28] Ephesians 5:22-33.

central and well-known text of the Old Testament as the ten commandments. The commandments are presented in the Scriptures not simply as a moral code but as an aspect of the covenant between God and his people. In the original language, the commandments are called the ten words rather than the ten commandments. The use of the term 'word' places the emphasis on their being about the relationship of God and his people: God speaks these words to his people.

The commandments begin with the phrase 'I am the Lord your God who brought you out of the land of Egypt, out of the house of slavery'. Thus they are placed within the context of the liberating activity of God for his people. And as the list of the 'words' goes on, they are all about God and God's people; they are words from God to his people. This comes out in the pronouns that are used: 'you shall not have strange gods before me', 'you shalt not kill', 'you shalt not commit adultery' and so on (Exodus 20:1-21; Deuteronomy 5:1-21).

These ten words are about God's continuing to be the one who delivers human beings from slavery. These words encourage what will continue to set them free and indicate those things that will return them to another form of slavery: Idolatry, murder, adultery, lying, etc. Underlying the commandments, the point is being made that it is God who liberates; whereas those things prohibited enslave.

Another critical element of the covenant and of the commandments is that the relationship with God cannot be separated from the relationships of human beings to each other. Relationship with God issues in right relationships between human beings. Religion and morality are essentially tied together in Israel's faith which was not the case with the other religions surrounding Israel at that time.

The stories of creation and the covenant

The story of the creation and the sin of Adam and Eve in the second and third chapters of the book of Genesis arises out of Israel's understanding of its failure in its relationship with God. The story reached its final version at a late stage in the development of Israel's tradition, that is at a late stage of Old Testament history and theology. This is an important point to make since it means that the story gathers up Israel's understanding of sin that had been developing in the centuries preceding its final draft. Therefore, the story can act as a sort of shortcut into that understanding of sin.

The stories of creation in the first three chapters of Genesis – and for that matter in all of its first eleven chapters – may be at the beginning of our Bibles but they are not at the beginning of the development of the biblical tradition. They were written much later and have been shaped by the religious history of Israel to which they give expression in their uniquely symbolic way. The actual infidelity of Israel to the covenant in the course of their history threw Israel off its true course. This infidelity in turn found expression in the narrative of the sin of Adam and Eve that shows them being thrown off their true course. The narrative reflects Israel's exile from its own land to Babylon in the expulsion of Adam and Eve from the garden of Eden. The exile to Babylon was interpreted by Israel as exile or expulsion from their land and so caused them to wonder if God had annulled his covenant with them. This fear began to change during the exile as the prophets urged the people to have faith in the fidelity of God. The shaping of the Adam and Eve narrative was also probably influenced by such events in the history of Israel as the infidelity of Solomon who was drawn into idolatry by his pagan wives, who were perhaps models for Eve.

These stories as we have them now have taken up ancient stories inherited from Israel's distant pre-covenant past and have been radically rewritten to express Israel's experience of their covenant with God and their own infidelity to that covenant.

Another theologically significant point in these stories is that they universalise Israel's experience of infidelity, suggesting that it mirrors the experience of all humankind. They do this in the very figures of Adam and Eve who are presented not just as the ancestors of Israel but of all human beings.

These stories are symbolic. They are not an attempt to give an historical account of humankind's beginnings. They seek to hold up a mirror to each and every generation of human beings so that they may discover within themselves what is presented in these stories. These narratives suggest that there is something missing or misshapen in humankind that in the final analysis consists in a missing or misshapen relationship with God. As symbolic narratives, these stories are highly relevant today.

These stories can be called mythic in the technical sense of that word. They are referred to as figurative in the

Catechism of the Catholic Church.[29] I have chosen to use the word symbolic because that word expresses more clearly the fact that they are given so that we may find an image of ourselves in them.[30]

As we have seen, these narratives take the history of Israel and extend it to all humankind in the figures of Adam and Eve, presenting these two figures as the first human beings. This projecting back to the beginnings is a way of saying that the matter being presented is relevant to all human beings, that what is being recounted can be found in some way in everyone and at every time. This ancient practice of projecting something back to the origins is a way of saying that the matter being presented is so much a part of the existence of human beings that it must always have been there.

Among other things, using the word symbolic for these narratives implies that the symbols used in them have their equivalents in other spheres of human life. They are symbols that may appear in dreams, poetry or art. And so our interpretation of them is parallel to our interpretation of such symbols as they appear in other fields.

These narratives present us with a series of symbolic figures. Adam's name comes from the name for earth or dust (*adamah*), Eve's name means mother of all the living.

---

[29] CCC, nos 289, 390.

[30] These stories are not suggesting that there was an original sin in the sense that a sin occurred at the beginning of human history whose effects have persisted throughout history. They are not about a first contaminating sin. These stories are providing images of the present situation of human beings in every generation.

Then there is the serpent, there are trees, there is nakedness, and, as can be the case in dreams, Adam and Eve find themselves blocked from getting to where they want to be. These are all symbolic images. Along with these, there are references to such other fundamental human realities as scapegoating, the arduousness of work, the pain of childbearing, the subjection of women to men.

In his study of symbolism, the French Christian philosopher Paul Ricoeur speaks of symbols not as thoughts but as things that give rise to thought.[31] That is – symbols cannot be reduced to ideas; rather they stir up ideas. We need to have this in mind as we interpret these narratives of Genesis. They suggest the origin of sin to us by means of the symbols entwined into the story. And because they are symbols, they do not present descriptions much less definitions but rather invite us to engage with them to discover something of our relationship with God, our relationships with each other and something about the causes of our involvement with evil. We need to see what these symbols mean in general among human beings and then in these inspired narratives; by so doing we seek to grasp something of our own present reality.

The symbols of the story of Adam and Eve

This story, even though later than most biblical references to sin, has been received within the Christian tradition as a major part of the Bible's response to the question of the

---

[31] Paul Ricoeur, *The Symbolism of Evil.* NY: Harper and Row, 1967, pp. 347-357.

origin of evil and human participation in it. It has had a very significant part to play in the history of the Christian understanding of sin.

We have seen that the story of Adam and Eve holds up to its readers images to be tried out on themselves, images that invite them to discover a dimension of themselves as individuals and of all other human beings. As we have seen, the authors of these narratives are deliberately suggesting a universal dimension to their work in the symbolic figures of Adam and Eve as the parents of all humankind. The authors are proposing that sin is not just something applying to an individual's situation but to humanity as a whole. This approach opens out readily enough to include what we would call today – in a different cultural context – social and structural sin.

The symbolic elements in the story are fascinating and compelling. I would like to highlight some of them that are important in the biblical understanding of sin.

The trouble begins with the snake. Snakes are not generally one of humanity's favourite animals and we tend to wonder at people who have the courage to befriend them. Snakes dwell in the undergrowth and are not obvious to sight; they slither and hiss and strike unexpectedly. In the common mind, they are poisonous, arousing the fear of death. We fear them. They appear in dreams, art, literature and religion with symbolic significance. When the story of Adam and Eve was written, they would already have had their place in the human imagination.

The responsibility for sin is not just sheeted home to Adam and Eve but also to the snake. Adam, Eve and the snake are caught up in the responsibility for this 'sin'. But who or what is the snake?

Paul Ricoeur suggests that the snake is a symbol of something within human beings that is not immediately obvious; it is there but hidden 'in the undergrowth'. The snake symbolises something present in and among human beings. It is part of them that is not on the surface. It slithers around inside them and among them.

Ricoeur follows on to suggest that in this imagery there is reflected the experience of temptation as something that seems external to human beings, as something that appears to come into them from outside. It embodies the experience of temptation that human beings do not initiate but which is present before they sin; it is there before they go along with it. It is something they give in to.

Evil is presented therefore as something to which they accede rather than something that they simply initiate. Responsibility for it, therefore, does not simply go back to Adam and Eve's choice – that is to say to human choices – but also to another force that is at work in them that they themselves have not put there and that seems to be outside of their immediate control. In sinning they go along with it.

This is reflected in the scapegoating that occurs between Adam, Eve and the serpent. Adam shifts the responsibility on to Eve, but also subtly onto God. Adam says 'The woman you gave to be with me, she gave me fruit from the tree and I ate it'. That is, he says that it is really the woman's fault and he is also implying that it was God's fault because it was he who gave him the woman. And Eve says 'The snake tempted me and I ate'. Is not this avoidance and passing on of responsibility an often-repeated feature of human behaviour?

Then there is the symbol of nakedness. 'Now both of them were naked, the man and his wife, but they felt no shame before each other' (Genesis 2:25). Adam and Eve discover that they are naked and because of this they are no longer at ease with each other, nor are they at ease with God. 'The man and his wife heard the sound of Yahweh God walking in the garden in the cool of the day and they hid from Yahweh God among the trees of the garden.' When asked why they were hiding, Adam responds: 'I was afraid because I was naked, and so I hid'. To which God replies: 'Who told you you were naked. Have you been eating from the tree I forbade you to eat?' (Genesis 3:8-12). They hide from God because they are naked. This is a powerful symbol of the vulnerability they have brought upon themselves, of the unease or 'dis-ease' they now feel with each other and with God.

The story symbolises two very different ways of being with God, implied in what was just said about nakedness. At first, we have the simplicity of God walking in the garden in the cool of the evening seeking the company of Adam and Eve – an image of ease between human beings and God. The serpent, however, suggests that God cannot be trusted, that God's real agenda is to frustrate human beings, to cut them down to size, to stop them being like gods. Does this not also echo a voice that whispers away in the human psyche that God is not trustworthy? This is the suggestion that suspicion is the surer way to approach God – and not just God but life in general. The misshapen relationship with

God imaged in this narrative reflects misshapen images of God in the human mind. Such images crop up frequently throughout human history and are present in the history of all human religions, just as they can be found in the history of Christianity.

All that Adam and Eve have – and so all that human beings have – has been received from God. This great story suggests that human beings want to be their own origin, that is they want what they are and have to be theirs exclusively without any acknowledgment that they are gifts that have been received. They want to take God's place and so their relationship with God is undermined. At the end of the narrative, they have lost that state of ease with God and are banished from the garden. They are cut off from the tree of life. They are unable to reach it any longer as they are blocked off from it 'by the Cherubim and the fiery flashing sword' (Genesis 3:22-24) that guard the way to the tree of life.

The tree of life is another significant symbol. It is the symbol of life being given and received, of life as a gift. And at the story's end, Adam and Eve are unable to get to it, that is to the source of life. There is a separation between them and the life-giving God, and the fruits of the earth now have to be hard won (Genesis 3:17).

Initially in the story, there is talk of two trees: the tree of life in the middle of the garden (Genesis 2:9; 3:22,24) and the tree of the knowledge of good and evil (Genesis 2:9, 15; 3:3,11). The two trees tend to coalesce as the story goes on. Is it intentional in this highly symbolic narrative to draw together the tree of life and the tree of the knowledge of good and evil? Does this coalescence present to us symbolically or mythically the idea that to sin is to cut yourself off from the source of life. A theology that drew sin and death together as both of them being separation from God would have been present in Israel before the time this story had reached its final form.

The narrative also pictures an enmity arising between human beings and creation as part of the loss of ease and harmony. The pain of childbearing and the domination of men over women are presented not as part of God's desire for human beings but as a result of their separation from God (Genesis 3:16). Human beings have to struggle to gain their food from the earth (Genesis 3:17-19). And death is seen as the fate human beings have brought upon themselves: 'dust you are and to dust you will return' (Genesis 3:19b).

This story is not just about separation between human beings and God, but about separations between human beings. Separation from God is seen as bringing about separation and conflict between human beings. The separation is symbolised by the rupture between Adam and Eve: 'Your yearning will be for your husband and he shall rule you' (Genesis 3:16b). There is separation between Adam and Eve and the earth: 'In pain you will get your food from it (the soil) all the days of your life' (Genesis 3:17b). The story of Adam and Eve is followed immediately in the Bible by the story of Cain and Abel, their sons, in which brother kills brother and the killer bears the burden of his act (Genesis 4:1-16). The rest of the first eleven chapters of the book of Genesis goes on to paint a picture of a humanity divided and in conflict.

At this point, it is good to recall something mentioned earlier in passing and that is that the theology of original sin that developed at a later date in Western Christianity was based on an historical interpretation of the Adam and Eve story. The presumption was that the story was speaking of an historical event of the past in which the two initial human individuals sinned. When speaking of original sin, what was then primarily intended was the historical sin of those first parents; and then the effects of that initial sin being passed on by them to the rest of humankind, all of whom were understood to be their descendants. The story being thus interpreted reversed the original purpose of the story that was to explain the presence of sin in the continuing history of human beings. The story of Adam and Eve was merely an instrument to explain that continuing history of human sinfulness.[32]

This historical interpretation of the story needs to be set aside. The story of Adam and Eve is our story; it intends to speak about humanity as it was in the past and as it is in the present. The story invites all human beings to discover themselves in it. It is a story about what John's Gospel would call the sin of the world. It is about that sinfulness that we find wherever human beings are to be found.

---

[32] In the theology of original sin, there were two forms of original sin described. The first was originating original sin (*peccatum originale originans*), that was the sin of Adam and Eve; the second was originated original sin (*peccatum originale originatum*), that was the sinfulness handed on to all of humankind as a result of the sin of Adam and Eve.

Chapter 4

Sin as Separation From God

The story of Adam and Eve in the book of Genesis presents in its symbolic way a view of the radical character of the relationship that human beings have with God. In doing so, it also presents a radical view of sin as separation from God, that is separation from the One who is the very source of all life.

In line with that perspective on the relationship between God and human beings, this story cannot be reduced to what it says about human sinfulness alone. The story of Adam and Eve's failure is a story within a larger story and that larger story sees human beings as being created by the breath of God being breathed into them (Genesis 3:7). That image of the breath of God in human beings implies an interior and intimate union between themselves and God.

In accordance with the symbolic and theological nature of these narratives, they do not mean to say that God only breathed the breath of life into human beings at the beginning of their existence but, rather, that God is constantly breathing the breath of life into them, even after a separation has come about between themselves and God.

Even in their state of separation from God, God does not abandon human beings but continues to open up new beginnings before his earthenware creatures who live because his breath is in them. These new beginnings find symbolic expression all through the following chapters of the book of Genesis. In the story, the sinful Adam and Eve found themselves before a new beginning, hard as it was to be (Genesis 3:20-24), so also Cain finds a new beginning after he murders his brother Abel (Genesis 4:12-16), and after the disaster of the flood, there is a new start for humanity (Genesis 8:15-20). And then comes the new divine initiative involving the choosing of a people to have a unique relationship with God within the world that is God's. This initiative begins with Abraham (Genesis 12:1-9) and continues not only through the rest of the book of Genesis but throughout the rest of the Bible up into the New Testament.

Each of these new beginnings takes its point of departure from the situation in which the figures find themselves or into which they have brought themselves. So there is no ignoring the wrong done or what human beings have brought upon themselves but a way ahead is offered, beyond that situation. Thus it is with the figures of Adam and Eve after their expulsion from the garden and with Cain after he has killed Abel.

Human goodness is likewise highlighted in the first story of creation (Genesis 1:1 to 2:4). This story was written later than the Adam and Eve story but is placed before it in the arrangement of the Bible as it has come down to us from those who compiled its various parts.[33] In this first chapter of the Bible, all that is created is said to be good and the creation of human beings is said to be very good (Genesis 1:31).

God created man and woman in the image of himself, male and female he created them (Genesis 1:27), thus conferring on them their unique dignity.

The living God does not fluctuate in his relationship to human beings, his word is everlasting and his love has no end. But that relationship is experienced differently by human beings once they have brought a distance from God upon themselves.

This separation, as we have seen, is not the result of an ancient or 'original' falling into sin, but of the mysterious state in which humankind finds itself in its historical existence. As we have seen, it was reflection on the historical experience of Israel's infidelity to God that was the fertile ground out of which these narratives grew and which was the catalyst for seeing that same infidelity to God in all humankind. The stories of the first eleven chapters of the book of Genesis offer symbolic insight into the present situation of humankind.

The point being made in these stories is that the relationship between God and human beings as it is experienced by human beings is not the easy or obvious relationship imaged in God's walking in the garden in the

---

[33] Scholars suggest that the final arrangement of the book of Genesis was done in Israel in the period following the Babylonian Exile that occurred in the sixth century before Christ.

cool of the evening as presented in Adam and Eve story; instead, a distance that has grown up between human beings and God. These narratives carry the implication that this state of separation from God leads to death, the ultimate separation from God. Separation from God is separation from life because life comes from God. As a consequence, humankind's state of sinfulness is seen to threaten its existence.

In the image of God

In the biblical and Christian vision, human beings are understood as being created in God's image. This vision is put forward in the first account of creation (Genesis 1:1 to 2:4): 'God created man in the image of himself, in the image of God he created him, male and female he created them' (Genesis 1:27). We need to remember that these words are the product of much prophetic and theological pondering that preceded them in Israel's history.

Separation from God, therefore, means that human beings are separated from the One in whose image they are made. And just as the image of a person refers back to that person for its authentication as an image, so human beings are authenticated by their innate relationship to God, the One in whose image they are made. Without that reference, they do not know who they really are; without that reference, they lose their anchor; without it, they are adrift, and so they are in a state of not being able to achieve their inbuilt specific purpose.

In the second creation account, humankind's profound link with God is expressed in a thoroughly symbolic way as we would expect of that narrative. This is the image spoken about in an earlier paragraph of God breathing life into Adam, his earthenware creature: 'The Lord God shaped man from the dust of the ground and breathed the breath of life into his nostrils, and the man became a living being' (Genesis 2:7). And then in accord with that same image at the end of the narrative, Adam is told 'By the sweat of your face shall you earn your food, until you return to the ground, for from there you were taken. For dust you are and to dust you shall return' (Genesis 3:19).[34]

God's initiative in the biblical revelation from Abraham onwards has been to bring human beings to the recognition of their innate relationship to God and of their innate – even if unrecognised – search for God. In the final redaction of the books of the Old Testament, the first eleven chapters of Genesis are placed before the story of the calling of Abraham. In that way they form a background to God's calling of Abraham by which God takes the initiative to create a new relationship with humankind. Abraham's call begins the forming of Israel as the People of God but, as we have seen, his call is seen as not just for Israel but for the whole of humankind (Genesis 12:1-3; 22:17; 26:4; Sirach 44:19-21).

---

[34] This imagery inspires the significance of the ashes on Ash Wednesday as the People of God begins its time of journeying to Easter where the new Breath of Life will be breathed into them by the Risen Jesus (John 20:22).

Sin and idolatry

We have already seen that the most significant sin in the Old Testament is idolatry – Israel's abandoning their covenant with God and going off after the gods of the peoples surrounding them. In so doing, Israel put something else between themselves and God, thus creating an obstacle to their relationship with God, creating a separation between themselves and God.

In putting anything else in the place of God, human beings bring a false direction upon themselves. They act as if they are made in the image of whatever idol they put in God's place and so are untrue to their own God-given nature. Since sin as such is a specifically and essentially religious notion, idolatry continues to be the model for sin.

Human beings tend to be shaped in the image of whatever it is they worship – whatever they *give themselves over to*. They become like their idols. Idols are made in the image of human fears, needs and desires. Idols – even though made in the image of human beings – in turn shape human beings in their own image. Idolatry is essentially narcissistic; it encloses human beings within themselves rather than opening them to the future and the transformation offered by being called into the image and likeness of God.

Idolatry turns God's plan on its head: in idolatry, the gods are made in the image of human beings. This is true not only of the idols of old but of those things that take their place in the contemporary world. Such things may be power, wealth, success, or even another person. Worship of any idol does not challenge us or beckon us forward, but encloses us in our own needs or desires. Belief in God can be reduced to a form of idol worship if it loses contact with the word of God. This last is a risk in all forms of religious fundamentalism, in which the mystery of God is ignored and God is reduced to being in the image of human beings.

The punishment of sin is not external to the sin. It is the outcome of the sin in which human beings become involved. The things worshipped have power in them and over them. Instead of worshipping the God in whose image they are made, they worship things not only less than God but less than themselves. The things that human beings are tempted to worship are like the snake in Ricoeur's interpretation of the narrative in Genesis: they tap into a hidden part of being human that is at work in human beings before any decisions or choices are made.

There is another significant consequence to the vision of human beings as made in the image of God. This finds expression in the Old Testament prohibition on making images of God. There were to be no statues of the God of Israel, because God was not image-able. This was a crucial element in the development of the revelation of God in Israel. The other nations had images of their gods. Such idols were to be anathema in Israel. It was regarding them that the prophets constantly warned and threatened Israel. God had set up his own image and that image is the human beings whom he created in his image and likeness.

In straying from the One in whose image they are made, human beings besmirch the image of God in themselves. This makes the true God obscure in our world. This is expressed in the story of Adam and Eve by the snake's suggestion that God has an agenda that is not for them but against them. The perception of God is distorted because they no longer see themselves as drawing life from the One who breathes the breath of life into them or as being made in the image of that same Living One.

Sin, as revealed in the Scriptures, is specifically and at its deepest level about a separation from God in the wake of which a separation between human beings themselves comes about. Sin is about falling out of contact and communion with God and each other.

Christ the true image of God

God shows God's true self in the coming of Christ. And over against the suggestion of the snake of the Adam and Eve story that God is against us, Christ's coming and the gift of himself to us in his death shows that God is indeed 'for us' and 'for all'. St Paul turns the snake's suspicious comment on its head when he says in his Letter to the Romans: 'If God is for us, then who can be against us? Since he did not spare his own Son, but gave him up for the sake of us all, will he not with him give us everything else?' (Romans 8:31-2). Christians do not believe in sin but in the redemption from sin given to humanity in Jesus Christ.

Significantly, in the context of our present presentation, Jesus is described as the perfect image of the God we cannot see.[35] The use of the term 'image' immediately relates him to every other human being, since all human beings are

---

[35] 2 Corinthians 4:4; Colossians 1:15-20; 3:10; Hebrews 1:1-4.

made in God's image. He is the way to finding the truth of God and so to finding the truth of being human and to overcoming the separation between God and human beings and between human beings themselves. He treads the path of reconciliation. The way of Jesus is not only the path to God but to the truth of ourselves. Jesus Christ is the perfect image of the God we cannot see, but in whose image we human beings are made.

As Christians, we believe in redemption from sin and death. We have discovered the One who enters into our human flesh and our human world, the One who did battle with this power of sin and by the strangest of means overcame it. By allowing human beings to bring him to death, he forced his way into our sinful humanity and by spreading out his arms on the cross – rather than taking up arms – he destroyed the power of sin and death to block our way to the tree of life. He introduced a stronger, ever-present, interiorly effective power into the world – yet a power that did not connive with sin by the use of discord and violence. In himself, he opened a new way for God to come into our world.

He broke through the barrier to the tree of life. He revealed and embodied the One who sent him to establish a new relationship with human beings. In Christian imagery, his cross is named the Tree of Life because in it we have access again to the One who is himself the Tree of Life. In Jesus Christ, the Tree of life is again in our midst; it is given to us. We can now eat of its fruit!

This Christian discovery of Jesus Christ and his breaking into our human world to bring God in among us in his new way is not just for those who believe but for all human beings. Christianity is the revelation of what God is also doing beyond its bounds. Christianity crystalises in itself the diffuse working of God in the whole of his creation, that creation into which he is constantly breathing life.

Sin and sins

In speaking of sin as separation from God, we need to emphasise again that we are speaking of a reality that goes beyond those human actions that are commonly called sins. There was wisdom in the traditional division of different degrees of sinfulness. In using the terms mortal sin and venial sin, a pastoral and theological point was being made that there were sins that had a serious effect on our relationship with God and others that did not. There also used to be talk of imperfections that were of even less account than venial sins. The very word 'imperfection' suggests that such things are simply part of the imperfect state in which human beings exist.

One problem with the above terms was that they limited sin to sinful human actions. So they dealt with 'sins' rather than 'sin', thus leaving out of play that deeper and more fundamental reality of a state of separation from God which, we have seen, is the more fundamental concern of the Scriptures.

Sin was described earlier in this book as human involvement in wrongdoing or evil. Such involvement can take many forms. There can be 'sinful' thoughts or feelings of many kinds that arise within us before we are even aware of them. Sinful actions can be slight or have serious and severe consequences; and they can have different degrees of deliberateness. Sinfulness can also simply be part of our belonging to a particular society or culture in which there are elements of inherent blindness; this brings to the fore the social and structural dimensions of sin. Sin can also be a fundamental handing over of oneself to the doing of evil, which is at the extreme end of the spectrum of sinfulness. There can even be the sin against the Holy Spirit (Matthew 12:31-32; Luke 12:10) that leaves no room for the activity of the Holy Spirit. Such a situation could be where the distinction between good and evil disappears and good is called evil and evil good.

To adequately take into account what the Scriptures see as sin, any instances of sin need to be placed within the context of the broader and deeper reality described therein – the sinfulness inherent in humankind. This is the mysterious presence of evil at work within that humankind which is also endowed with great goodness.

Human actions are related to the ambiguity of goodness and sinfulness in human beings. Sinful actions, thoughts or omissions manifest this deeper sinfulness and increase its influence among human beings. Good attitudes and actions diminish its influence among human beings. This deeper sinfulness can be called 'the sin of the world'.

The term 'the sin of the world' that we find in the Gospel of John and that is mentioned frequently in the celebration of the Eucharist sees all the sinfulness of the world tied together as an organic interacting whole. The individual sinfulness of human beings, the perpetration of great evils, the social structures that are distorted are all seen as part of the condition in which human beings find themselves.

This situation is often imaged in terms of light and darkness. Light, like goodness, is a positive thing; darkness, on the other hand, like sin, is negative: darkness does not really have a reality of its own, it is an absence of light. This is how sin is seen in comparison to goodness. Sin comes about where human beings are at odds with God, the Holy One.

That separation of human beings from God does not come about by God's withdrawal from the relationship but by means of the straying of human beings from the One in whose image they are made, and this distorts their being God's image. God is unendingly faithful. He will always seek out those who have strayed. The great instance of his coming to seek out his strays is the coming of his Christ, his anointed One, among us.

It is interesting that the phrase 'the sin of the world' is almost always used when speaking about Christ who takes it away. He is the one who penetrates it, falls victim to it and rises out of it, thus bringing its power to separate us from God to an end precisely because he is Emmanuel, God-with-us. And it is to the image of Christ as 'the Lamb of God' that the phrase 'the sin of the world' is attached. The lamb whose shed blood (his death) will deliver human beings from the bondage of this 'sin of the world' (see Exodus 12:21-28). The Lamb of God who took the burdens of humanity upon himself and was led to the slaughter but has the nations for his heritage (see Isaiah 52:13 to 53:12).

It is important to see these deeper dimensions of what we mean by sin as the context within which we understand the significant sins that individuals commit. It is important to distinguish the two and to relate them.

Which Image of God?

Having spoken of human beings as made in the image and likeness of God and having looked at sin as a disturbance of that relationship, we also need to be aware of the images of God that are in fact to be found among human beings and in human cultures. And so the reason for the title of this section: 'Which Image of God?' and that title could also be changed a little to: 'The Image of Which God?' The way in which people imagine God has great impact on their belief in God or their lack of it and so consequently on the way in which sin and forgiveness are conceived.

We need to be attentive to what is evoked in people's minds by the word 'God', especially in a secular situation in which evangelisation is on the Church's agenda. There can be very real religious difficulties with the way in which human beings imagine God without this necessarily being any fault of their own. Images of God are often conveyed to individuals within a culture or by inadequate or simplistic concepts of God, which can be conveyed by poor religious teaching and preaching.

We cannot avoid using images for God because we are unable to think or speak about God without using images taken from the visible and tangible world around us. But none of these images can pretend to represent God as God is. It is beyond the capacity of the human mind to do so. We always need to be aware that in speaking of God we are using images, as we also need to be aware of the point of reference of these images in our everyday world. For example, when we call God 'Father', we are using an image that in the first place refers to fatherhood as we know it in our experience. That image needs not only purification in order to use it to speak about God but also needs to be used in the awareness that it applies and at the same time does not apply to God! God is always immeasurably more than we can speak of or imagine.

There are images given in the Scriptures which the biblical tradition consecrates by its continual and developing use of them. This development reaches its culmination in the very person of Jesus Christ who is the perfect image of the God we cannot see, and whom John describes as God's very word in our flesh and blood, that is God's expression of himself in our flesh and blood (John 1:14). That image and that word, Jesus Christ, is the translation of God into our humanity. Jesus Christ is himself the medium in which God shows Godself to us.

So the images of God throughout the Old Testament are part of a continuing process of development culminating in Jesus Christ. They, therefore, need to be interpreted in terms of that movement towards the Christ. This is a process that involves a re-interpretation of those images and at times requires the setting aside of some of those images.

It is not just the images of God given in the biblical tradition that need to find their culmination in Jesus Christ, but also the images that are present in our own minds, wherever those images have originated. Such images need to be in dialogue with the biblical revelation in its progression towards Jesus Christ. Thus the importance of our developing understanding of and dialogue with the Scriptures.

Listening to and reading the Scriptures does need to be a dialogue, a listening and an honest responding. The images of God that are at work in our minds and hearts all need to be filtered through the rediscovery of God in Jesus Christ. Continuing listening to and responding to the Scriptures in the gathered community of the Church, along with a personal and internal dialogue with them, is an integral part of the Christian life.

If we were to look at the images of God throughout the history of the Christian tradition, we would find therein many and varied images, some of which would be more in tune with the image of God revealed to us in Jesus Christ, than others would be, which is also the case in the history of Christian art and literature.

A current, common image of God

There are images of God embedded in human cultures that are profoundly misleading because they misrepresent the relationship of human beings to God as ultimately revealed in the life, death and resurrection of Jesus Christ.

This is true of some of our current Western cultural presuppositions. In recent centuries in these cultures, there has been a quite dominant image of God that has also had its influence in the minds of believers.

From the Enlightenment in the seventeenth century on, there has been a prominent image of God as the divine architect or the first mover of the world but who then steps back from the world and leaves it to its own devices, without being in any way present in its ongoing development.

This image arose in tandem with the belief that the world was autonomous and could be explained in terms of its own internal workings without reference to any immediate intervening of God's creative activity. This attitude was very important in the development of science. The new sense of the autonomy of the world is an accurate and fruitful insight into the world. Many of the disputes that arose between the Church and those who held to this view of the autonomy of the world had the effect of blocking the development of a renewed image of God that gelled with that new mindset. And that new mindset has proved to be a potent influence in the shaping of the modern Western world.

For some who continued to believe in God in this new cultural mindset, the law of God became the important or even the only link between God and his world. God's law remained relevant and obedience to his laws became the fundamental expression of 'faith'.

This brought about a situation that is relevant to the understanding of sin. This centrality of the law of God has had a formative influence on the way sin has been conceived as an infringement of God's law. It gave credibility to the legal approach to sin and the sacrament of penance. It presented God as a lawgiver and judge with whom our major link was his law and our obedience to that law.

Although the Scriptures often speak of God as directly intervening in the workings of the world and tend to ignore the reality of the this-worldly causes of things, there is a deeper vein to be tapped in the Scriptures that sees God's creativity at work at its own divine creative level without this creativity being in competition with the observable causes of things.

In every age, there has been the need to renew our images of God, that was often accompanied by objections from those opposed to such a renewal. This renewing of our images of God cannot be achieved simply by having recourse to the culture of the time but has to come about in dialogue with the revelation of God in the biblical tradition.

The common image of God in relation to the world over recent centuries has tended to be an image of God as extrinsic to the world. This was the way in which God's transcendence – that is God's being beyond the created world – was imagined. However, God's relationship to the world can be understood differently. That relationship can be seen in terms of God's being the inner source of the world's being, the creator who is always bringing it to life, as the fountain from which life and being spring. This does not confuse God and the world but sees God as the One who is the ultimate and continuing source of the world's being, the wellspring of its own innate creativity. The poet Gerard Manley Hopkins speaks of the deep down creativity in things, which we might call the trace of God the Creator in it. This is quite coherent with the biblical recognition of God as personal and yet unnameable in his mystery. As one theologian puts, it God is both 'with us' and 'in us'.[36]

---

[36] Xavier Thevenot, 'Quelques clarifications sur la théologie du péché', in Louis-Marie Chauvet et Paul De Clerck (dir), *Le Sacrement du Pardon entre hier et demain*. Paris: Desclee, 1993, 141-3. Also for an excellent presentation of the difference between God's influence in the world and that of ordinary

Such an image of God as the inner source of life enables us to understand more clearly the scriptural vision of sin as something that separates human beings from God and so from the life that comes from him. And it makes sense of the scriptural pairing of sin and death.

---

finite causes, see Rowan Williams, *Christ. The Heart of Creation*. London, NY, Oxford, New Delhi, Sydney: Bloomsbury Continuum, 2018, esp. pp. 1-26.

Chapter 5

Sin: A Human Reality

U p to this point, we have been looking at sin as it is presented in the Scriptures. However, what is being described in those writings is an identifiable part of human existence as it has been experienced by men and women personally and socially throughout the ages and in the present time. The aim of this chapter is to identify in everyday life the reality that the Scriptures describe as sin from their specifically religious perspective. The scriptural account of sin is not something that the biblical authors have dreamed up; rather, it is an integral part of their interpretation of human life.

Even a scant knowledge of human history makes us aware of the ravages that human evildoing has brought about in the past, just as it is an obvious part of human existence as we know it at the present time. As an egregious instance of such evil, the terrors brought about by Nazism before and during the Second World War continue to have their effects today and continue to live in the memory of so many people. They have become a paradigm of evil for the generations of the post-World War II period. And Nazism is only one instance of human beings perpetrating great evil on each other; countless other less well known instances of such evil have occurred in the past and continue to occur in the present. And the consequences of such evils continue to haunt the people who have suffered from them and to question the humanity of those who have perpetrated them.

For our purposes in this book, we have been describing sin as human involvement in wrongdoing or evil. In common parlance, the word sin is still used as a way of describing evils without that usage having the theological overtones that have been described in earlier chapters of this book.

In speaking about human involvement in evil, we need to see it as only one element in the complexity of human existence; human goodness is one of its equally present and persistent characteristics. Realistically, we need to acknowledge that human beings are ambiguous; there is in human beings both great goodness and a capacity for doing evil that can be fearfully destructive. In pondering the life we live and life as we see it around us, we can see so much goodness and so many people who inspire and encourage us. And yet on the other hand, we can witness things that make us wonder about the self-centredness and capacity for lesser and greater evil in human beings. We can be aware of things that make us recoil in horror and make us wonder if the evils that bedevil humanity can ever be overcome.

And are there not also moments when we catch an echo of such things within ourselves? Human beings are ambiguous: there is so much goodness and yet there is some sort of recurrent inclination to evil.

Self-centredness

One way to identify in concrete human life what the Scriptures and the tradition call sin is to start with a basic experience that we find at work within ourselves. That experience is self-centredness. This is not selfishness as such but that centredness on ourselves which is part of us, which is an automatic reaction within us, which we cannot help but experience. It is there within us before we are even aware of it. We discover it only by reflection on our motives, our actions and the spirit in which we live our lives.

St Augustine speaks of this self-centredness as a turning in on ourselves, by doing which we turn away from God and from other people. He uses the Latin phrase 'curvatio in seipsum', which we can translate as turning in on ourselves, or perhaps using the image captured within Augustine's phrase, a 'curving into ourselves'.

Is not our first spontaneous reaction to things or events a concern for its effect on myself or on those who are 'mine'? Even before we think about it, do we not find that spontaneous reaction at work within us? This is especially noticeable – and unavoidable – in our perception of danger.

On the broader scale, are not governments, businesses, trade unions, scientific institutions, churches, nations, spontaneously tempted to think first of their own interests, that is their own self-interest? Does not this temptation seem to be virtually universal? Is it even escapable?

This centredness on oneself is not in itself a matter of personal sin; there is no question of attributing guilt for it.

Initially, it is not even conscious or deliberate. It is simply there within us. It is part of the complexity of who we are.

But is it this self-centredness the ground in which sin germinates? Self-centredness can turn into selfishness in which the self becomes the centre of everything. It can become a deliberate centring of everything on oneself to the detriment of what this might do to others. Everything can become so centred on the self that nothing or no-one else matters. This self-centring can be all-absorbing.

Perhaps the ancient trio of serious sins from the first centuries of Christianity epitomise this self-centredness become selfishness. Idolatry ties up human beings into themselves; it distorts their fundamental orientation to go beyond themselves. Murder is a radical manifestation of this centring on the self: someone who impedes my way ahead or threatens me has to be removed. And adultery – at its most serious – refuses commitment and fidelity in the realm of crucial human relationships.

And war! It is war that brings to the surface the ultimate social manifestation of this centredness upon the self. In war, everything is galvanised to protect 'ourselves' and to overcome or even annihilate those who have become nothing more than the 'enemy'. Even though war may sometimes be unavoidable, it brings about a radical self-centring for survival. War releases a multitude of fearful and unforeseeable evils that continue even after the war itself has come to an end.

War also brings out the reality that there are, at times, unavoidable situations in which self-centredness cannot but hold sway! In the face of the unjust and violent aggressor pushing for war, human beings can be constrained to make choices between greater and lesser evils – and, in the case of war, the lesser evil can be terrifyingly great! These are situations in which the depth of conflicted separated-ness among human beings proves inescapable. We can all find ourselves in situations in which there is an inevitability to our being bound up in self-centredness.

This centredness upon self is part of the human condition. It is not just about the attitudes and actions of individuals but about what it is like to be human. It tends to break up human communion; it leads human beings to pull apart from one another and even to pull each other apart.

Alongside this self-centredness, we find the natural human tendency to reach out to others. We are made for relationship; we become ourselves in relationship. This is true from our earliest days: from birth onwards, are we not reaching out to and enjoying others? This directedness and responsiveness to others is a counterbalance to the tendencies grounded in self-centredness.

Self-centredness is not the right path for human beings who are made for others and for whom relationship to others is crucial for wellbeing. Self-centredness has ultimately destructive effects.

Marriage and family provide one of the basic human social structures that invite human beings out of their self-centredness into centring on others. We can see this in the love of so many married couples and in the self-giving and constant love and care of parents for their children. But this love is achieved at a cost, at a going beyond oneself in a costly love. In the same sphere of family life, we can also see the effect of self-centredness becoming selfishness where one or both partners are not prepared to move out of their self-centredness into a self-giving relationship or in the care of their children. And, so often, further separation and conflict arise as a result of such refusals.

We can also witness this passage out of self-centredness into self-giving in so many admirable human beings. In the light of Christ's gospel, we see the Spirit of God at work in all such people, whatever their beliefs. But alongside such admirable human beings, we can also see others whose lives are marked by grasping as much as they can for themselves, or reducing others to instruments for their own success or advantage.

Human sinfulness is complex, social and structural

Human beings become who they are socially. Each unique person is born into a formative network of human beings and into a particular society and its culture. This is so from the first days of everyone's life as radically dependent and highly receptive and 'absorbent' infants. Each person absorbs from their parents, family and society ways of seeing the world and ways of living life that form them as persons and shape the way they see the world. This all happens pre-consciously and it is all the more powerful for being so. Societies and cultures tend to make the individuals within them in their own image.

Language is a powerful illustration of this. Languages have their own distinct way of taking a hold on reality, that is their own way of seeing the world. And the native languages of people are absorbed unconsciously by those who speak them. They are taken in by and take possession of human beings.

Being such profoundly social beings, human beings receive from their social ambience both a slice of the riches of humanity and of the failings of humanity in the course of their personal coming to be. Both the goodness and love surrounding them and the blindness and distortion that is part of their social atmosphere are given entry into each person in this profoundly social formation. Self-centredness is a part of this inheritance just as is the capacity to give of oneself.

This deep social dependence does not take away human freedom but situates it and gives it shape. It gives it an interactive context. Human freedom is not absolute, nor is the human individual an isolated monad. Human freedom is formed by the influences that have shaped it. Human beings become who they are as individuals out of the fundamental formative influences of parents, family, social and cultural and religious traditions. They can also come to identify these influences, accept them and enjoy them, just as they can be critical of them and find the capacity to go beyond them.

Human individuals can, therefore, do wrong or evil. But this happens within a context, within a situation that is at least to some extent distorted. It happens within what we have called – from a faith perspective – the sinfulness of the world that is one aspect of what is absorbed in the course of becoming a human being.

Human attitudes and actions give expression to this deeper sinfulness. As stated earlier, good actions decrease this sinfulness and bad actions reinforce it.

One element of this complex inheritance is the breakdown of human communion. Self-centredness-become-selfishness pulls against communion between human beings, separating them from each other.

Breakdowns of human communion occur throughout human societies and affect individuals interiorly and exteriorly. Such breakdowns in human communion occur not only in the lives of individuals but between groups, races and nations. When hurt or injustice is done to any group or people, there is a reaction within that group that inevitably works away inside them bringing about suspicion, anger and often violence. Such reactions have been aroused, for instance, by the presumed superiority of one people or group of people over another as is manifested in class snobbery, imperialism and in racism. All of these human evils leave their mark on the people who are victimised by them and on the humanity of the victimisers. Such things fall back on one group of people being so centred on themselves, either implicitly or explicitly, that others cease to matter.

Even when human beings seek to work together, human self-centredness rears its head. As an example, the United Nations Organisation was set up to enable human beings to work together and to avoid conflict but its work is under constant pressure because of the self-interest of the various powers involved in it who so often pull against each other. The aim of the UN is to seek to substitute cooperation for competition but this aim is constantly under threat from the self-interest of the political powers working within it.

Self-centredness has self-multiplying effects. As a person or a group or a nation retreats into self-centredness, it can cause other concerned parties to do the same in self-defence. To mention again the Second World War, we can see in its beginnings a classical example of such an interaction. As Nazism became more and more powerfully centred on its self-aggrandisement, it spread its attitudes among the German people in such a way that war eventually became inevitable. There came to be no way out of conflict and so other nations saw themselves as having no choice but to go to war in self-defence and in defence of values that they saw as essential to human wellbeing.

And Nazism in Germany did not come out of nowhere. The reparations imposed on Germany at the end of the First World War were so crippling that they formed part of the fertile ground in which Nazism could germinate. Those reparations were in turn imposed by nations who had been afflicted by the ravages of an earlier war and so they came to seek reparation and perhaps revenge.

The above is an example of a chain of causes and effects at work that keeps the reality of human evildoing rolling on and affecting generation after generation. And there is no simple moral solution to this ongoing evil. Simple resolutions to 'do the right thing' are not permanently effective. The suspicion, mistrust and breakdowns keep cropping up, despite good intentions.

The Scriptures would interpret this human situation in terms of a humankind which has lost its anchor in God in whose image it is made. Having cut itself loose from God, it cannot find a point of unity and so becomes scattered and unable to find a sufficient source of communion. Ultimately, it is centredness on self that takes the place of God, whatever guise that new idol may take. The 'other things' that are being sought are related to the centredness on self which human beings find within themselves.

All of the above leads to the Christian conviction that humankind is in need of someone who will set them free from the bonds that seem to hold them captive – it is in need of a Redeemer!

Sin and the Gospel

The call of the gospel is crucial to this situation. In the gospels, Jesus calls human beings to conversion. His call to human beings is to go beyond themselves, which is the very meaning of the word conversion. His call is not just a call to change our attitudes and actions but to change the way we see things and to do so in the light of the new discovery of God that he embodies. Jesus calls human beings and enables them to move out of separation from God into union with God, that always involves a going beyond themselves.

Jesus gives himself utterly to the very point of death but at a cost (Matthew 26:36-46; Mark 14:32-42; Luke 22:29-36; John 12:20-36). He reverses the self-centredness that is in human beings into a self-giving that is complete. He brings the energy of a self-giving love into the world – which love is beyond the capacities of human beings.

We human beings live in a tension. It is a tension between self-centredness that can drag us away from others and from God and the Spirit of God supporting us and working within us to take us beyond ourselves to others and to God. Both that self-centredness and that Spirit have power within us.

This living tension is not restricted to those who explicitly follow Christ. Christ's Spirit is at work wherever we find the qualities of the Beatitudes lived out among human beings, whoever those human beings may be and whatever they may believe. His Spirit is at work wherever we see happening among human beings what is described in the *Preface of the Second Eucharistic Prayer of Reconciliation* that gives thanks for God's presence and action in the world. It prays 'In the midst of conflict and division, we know it is you who turn our minds to thoughts of peace. Your Spirit changes our hearts: enemies begin to speak to one another, those who are estranged join hands in friendship, and nations seek the way of peace together. Your Spirit is at work when understanding puts an end to strife, when hatred is quenched by mercy, and vengeance gives way to forgiveness'.

It is in the light of the words and actions of Jesus in the gospels that the working of his Spirit in the world can be discerned, recognised and supported.

The gospel concerns sin. It concerns the healing of this state of separation from the One in whom alone human beings can ultimately find their true selves. The separation from God in human beings is bridged in the coming of Emmanuel: the God who is with us, who has taken his place among us. Jesus is the one who is the perfect image of the God we cannot see. He has broken into the state of separation from God in which humanity exists: he has brought God in among us. His resurrection out of the death that was imposed on him by human beings brought his Spirit into the whole world. And that Spirit is constantly at work, bridging the separation between human beings and God. Whatever the situation in which human beings find themselves, God's Spirit is at work among them.

The Spirit of the redeeming and reconciling God is always at work ,seeking to entice us out of self-centredness into going beyond ourselves to the other – both the human other and the divine Other.

Chapter 6

Christ and Sin

A s we have seen, sin involves more than making bad choices and the effects that proceed from those choices. Sin cannot be reduced to the sinful acts, thoughts or omissions of individuals. To do this would be to reduce the overall reality of the sinfulness we have been speaking about to particular instances that manifest that sinfulness. To limit our awareness of sin to such instances alone is to let lie hidden the deeper reality of sin brought to light in the biblical tradition. That tradition culminates in the coming of Jesus of Nazareth into a human society with the effects which that coming had on that society and individuals within it. His coming involves the climax of God's self-revelation, and it brought human sinfulness out into the light of God.

Sinfulness comes out into the open in the conflicts between Jesus and those who seek his death. All of the people whose choices and decisions brought about the death of Jesus are acting not only as individuals but are giving expression to forces that are at work in their social and political situation. These same forces are at work in all human situations in one way or another. They concretise the sin of the world. And when John's Gospel uses the phrase 'the sin of the world', we need to note that the word used for sin in that phrase is in the singular not the plural: the word is 'sin', not 'sins' (John 1:29). All the actions that brought about Jesus' death shared the characteristic of being subject to and acceding to the evil that is capable of enticing human beings into its thrall. It is that evil symbolised by the snake in the story of Adam and Eve.

The Father raising Jesus out of the death that was imposed on him by human beings revealed that what was at play in his death was not just a conflict between Jesus and those involved in his death but between God and those same people and institutions. By raising Jesus out of death, the Father took a stand for him and against whatever brought about his death.

It is in the resurrection of Jesus that we have the ultimate revelation of sin, that is of what is out of line with God. Sin is revealed in its being overcome! In the light of Jesus' death and resurrection, there is revealed to us what is in accord with God and what is not. God stood with Jesus and not with those whose attitudes and actions led to his condemnation and killing. The sin involved was not just the action of individuals but was an expression of the complex social atmosphere of the time and of its political, religious and popular structures.

Entangled in the sin of the world

Jesus Christ became entangled in the sinfulness of the human situation. He took his place as a human being in human history and was subject to all that human beings are

95

subject to. So taking his place in human history meant that he was subject to that strand of human history which is its involvement in wrongdoing and evil.

Jesus Christ brought into our world a previously unknown attachment to the Father, to the One who is the fountain from which human beings and all of creation springs. His attachment to the Father was such that sin – that is separation from God – had no hold on him. He was, as the Letter to the Hebrews says, like us in all things but sin (Hebrews 4:15). His relationship to the Father in its utter uniqueness excluded sin but did not exclude the experience of temptation as the Gospels (Matthew 4:1-11; 26:36-46; Mark 1:12-13;14:32-42; Luke 4:1-13; 22:40-46) and the Letter to the Hebrews make clear (2:18; 4:14-15).

Personally sinless though he was, he did not withdraw from the sinful situation of the world in which he lived out his life. His personal sinlessness did not withdraw him from the effects of human sinfulness in his social situation or from the influence of the human institutions that were part and parcel of his life.

He lived out his human life there and then in his own time and place and in the midst of all the forces that shaped human beings and their conduct at that time. Among these forces were those arising from human weakness and sinfulness as is the case in every human historical situation. He encountered a selection of the same forces that all human beings encounter in their own particular time and place. He lived out his life in engagement with these forces in his own slice of history as we do in ours.

His entanglement in human affairs meant that he encountered in those around him attitudes and actions that were inconsistent with his unique and radical relationship with the Father and the Father's purposes for the world. Thus he met with some enthusiastic responses, some acceptance, some indifference and finally with rejection.

The powers that be

He engaged with 'the powers that be' as they were in his world at that time. He was taken before Pontius Pilate, a Roman governor. He stood before a tribunal of one of the most significant empires the world has known. Whatever its achievements, it was an empire that came to be through unrelenting violence and was successful on the back of slavery and oppression. Christ stood before this power to which the individual person meant little.

Roman governors also belonged to a caste of people who lived in a world of ambition. They were part of an Empire-wide system in which people crawled over one another in order to promote their careers and their family prospects. In Pilate, Jesus came up against the power of this over-riding ambition.

He was subject to the background influence of the insurgents who resorted to violence to set Israel free. These insurgents against the Roman occupation had a considerable influence on his situation in that their recurrent violence set the stage for further potential conflict between the Roman occupiers and the people of Israel. And just as the potential recurrence of violence puts the forces of law and order on edge today, so it did then. The influence of the insurgents in the background could give credibility to the accusation that Jesus was a danger to society and a source of further insurrection.

He engaged with the religious powers of his time and their attachment to and absolutising of their religious attitudes and the religious establishment of the time. He came into conflict with them in the name of God his Father, whom they also claimed as their God.

He got caught up in the power of the mob in its fickleness, many of whom seemed to be enthusiastic in their response to him until he did not turn out to be the sort of Messiah they could recognise or desire; and so they turned aside from him and then against him.

He chose and engaged constantly with disciples who struggled to take his words to heart and who, like the crowds, sought to make of him the sort of Messiah they wanted. And so they melted away at the critical time. He engaged with Peter who was truly attached to Jesus but whose fear for himself led him into denying him. He encountered the betrayal of a friend, Judas Iscariot, 'who had shared his bread' but who, unlike Peter, could not go beyond his guilt and turn back to Jesus.

Jesus was entangled in all of this. He brought his relationship to the Father into all of this to the extent that those who were in conflict with him were in conflict with God. His entanglement in these human situations involved the entanglement of God in these human situations.

He was executed as a criminal. He was a possible insurgent to the Romans. He was a blasphemer to the

Jewish authorities, and he was so precisely because of his relationship to the Father. He became what his society considered 'the sinner'. St Paul says Jesus became sin for us (2 Corinthians 5:21). And so he was excluded, rejected, cast out and killed which was the fate his accusers considered necessary for sinners.

But he who became sin for us was proclaimed as the Holy One by the Father's act of raising him out of the death imposed on him by human beings. The image of his being seated at the right hand of the Father is the image of his being God's representative, God's chosen one, the one who truly stood on the side of God.

Wonderfully – in God's strange ways – humanity became something new in the resurrected Jesus. The non-violent God turned the tables on evil. Human beings were gifted with being set free and being glorified in their relationship to the God in whose image they are made.

Death and sin are defeated in this paradoxical way, in this unarmed and radically self-giving response of God to human violence and human sinfulness.

Killed by human attitudes and actions, by the interplay of so many forces – forces that in different forms are still active among us today – he is raised out of death into the glory of the Father. Despised, rejected, considered of no account by his contemporaries, he has become the way in which new life and a new future passes over into our world.

Not only then but now

Two crucial points need to be made in order to understand the significance of the encounter between Jesus and human beings in their sinfulness. First, as already touched on, those forces with which Jesus was entangled were not only forces of his time, they are forces which in other forms are at work in all times and in our present time. Their equivalents are part of every age. Jesus lives in the midst of one expression of those forces that were concretised in Pontius Pilate, in the mob, in the religious authorities, in the insurgents, in the violence of the Roman army, in the weakness of Jesus' disciples, and in the very human attitude of 'wanting what we want' that meant that Jesus was not seen as fulfilling what was commonly expected of the one who was to be the Messiah.

We can identify all those same forces at work in parallel people, crowds, institutions and structures today. They are doing to human beings now what was done to Jesus then. His victory is not just over the human sinfulness of his time but of those same forces in every time.

Father, forgive them...

Secondly, Luke's Gospel gives us words of Jesus on the cross that are to the point here: 'Father, forgive them; they do not know what they are doing' (Luke 23:34). These are not merely pious words; they fit into one of the important threads of Luke's Gospel – that of God's forgiveness.

'They do not know what they are doing.' We must not reduce the account of Jesus' death to simplistic opposites in which Jesus is 'the goodie' and those involved in his death 'the baddies'. Those words of Jesus on the cross recognise the evil that is afoot but calls for the Father's forgiveness because those killing him are blind to what they are really doing. Those bringing about his death are both perpetrators and victims – victims of forces they do not fully recognise. They are victims of the anger and violence that arise when one people oppresses another. They are victims of the political compromise which the Jewish leaders had worked out with the Romans whose purpose was to stall further violence and oppression. They were victims of human insecurity that so often distorts religious faith into something idolatrous. They are victims of their own fears and desires.

There are so many 'blinding' factors at work in such human situations that so often make human beings people 'who do not know what they are doing', even while doing real evil. This does not cancel the reality that human beings are capable of doing great evil with open eyes, but it does bring into such situations the surprising wonder of the redeeming action of the God who is love, and who is among us in Jesus the Christ.[37]

The creative power of God that is blocked by human sinfulness is released in the love of Christ going to his death and is manifested in his resurrection. This is what the creative power of God has done and can do in human beings. Christ's resurrection was the full manifestation of

---

[37] There are many scriptural references to blindness and – associated with that to darkness and the night which disable human beings from seeing – as images of the influence of sin. See for example, Proverbs 4:18-19; Psalms 17:29; 106:10-11; Isaiah 59:9-10; John 1:5; 3:19-21; 8:12, 31-34, 9:4; 11:10, 13:30; 1 John 5:10; 2:11; 3:5. As Judas leaves the Supper, John tells us 'It was night' (13:30). And at the death of Jesus, darkness came over the earth (Luke 23:44).

God's creative power (his kingdom, his reigning) that had already been made concrete in the miracles of Jesus' lifetime. The unique relationship to the Father that Jesus brought into the human world bursts into flower in the resurrection.

The Lamb of God

We have already referred to the second part of the phrase 'the Lamb of God who takes away the sin of the world', but the title 'the Lamb of God' given to Christ in this phrase is significant and the image captures symbolically the person and work of Christ that has been presented in this chapter.

Lambs were a crucial part of the religious rituals of Israel. They were central to so much of what went on in the temple; they were the dominant sacrificial victims of Jewish worship.[38] And they were, of course, at the centre of the celebration of the Passover as its central symbol and sacrificial component. The Passover was not just a matter of what went on in the temple but what went in the homes of the people of Israel at that great feast.

The lamb at Passover was particularly significant because its use was not just about what the priests did in the temple, but of what the people did in their homes. The paschal lamb was before their eyes and in their hands. Their celebration involved their very concrete and hands-on dealing with the Passover Lamb that also had such religious and theological meaning.

---

[38] The sacrifice of lambs was involved in morning and evening burnt offerings, the first day of the month, all seven days of Passover and the feast of weeks.

Lambs were seen as innocent, pure and gentle. They were led to the slaughter as innocents for no fault of their own but precisely because of their innocence, purity and gentleness.

It is also suggested that there was an implicit sense of efficaciousness associated with sacrificial lambs because in the Old Testament sacrificial system, it was largely through them that reconciliation and union with God was achieved.[39]

This is all background to the title 'Lamb of God' being given to Jesus. He is the innocent one who takes away the sin of the world, that is who bridges the separation between human beings and God –separation as the ultimate biblical understanding of sin.

In John's Gospel, the Baptist refers to Jesus as 'the lamb of God' twice (1:29, 35). In the overall plan of John's Gospel, we need to see this title linked to John 18:28 and 19:14, 31. In these passages, it is noted that the trial and death of Jesus takes place on the day of preparation for the Passover. It was in the afternoon of that day on which Jesus was crucified that the Passover lambs were being immolated in the temple. As well as that, John emphasises that the legs of Jesus were not broken on the cross (19:33, 36) which was part of the ritual requirements concerning the paschal lamb (Exodus 12:46). So, from the beginning to the end of his Gospel, John is portraying Jesus as the Lamb of God who takes away the sin of the world.

---

[39] See *The Interpreter's Dictionary of the Bible*. Vol.3. Nashville/ NY: Abingdon Press, 1962, p. 58 'Lamb'.

Jesus is the Paschal Lamb of the New Testament, the one in whom union between human beings and God is brought about, the one in whom sin is overcome.

Chapter 7

Identifying Sin in the Light of the Gospel

I n the preceding chapter, we looked at the revelation of
sin in the death and resurrection of Jesus. This invites us
to be aware that wherever we see other instances of the
same forces at work that led to the death of Jesus, there we
can discover human sinfulness at work. Wherever we can
identify attitudes among human beings that are the same
as those which were in conflict with the attitudes of Jesus,
there we can name sin.

The purpose of this book is not to list sins or to consider
their particular gravity or lack of it but to emphasize those
elements of the gospel that enable us to shift our core
understanding of sin from 'sins' to 'sin', that is from sinful
human actions alone to an understanding of sin as an aspect
of humankind's condition.

To refer to the quotation from James Keenan used earlier
in this book, our interest is 'in the fact and pervasiveness
of sin as well as its roots in the human condition and our
social structures'. We can begin to do this by looking at the
account of the woman taken in adultery in John's Gospel
(8:2-11). The woman's accusers are quite clearly identifying

her as the one who is the sinner and themselves as being not only the righteous, but her judges. But how does Jesus see sin in this passage? How does he embody the attitude of God to the people in that scene? The telling of that story as a part of the gospel puts before us a clear instance of Jesus' dealing with sin and the sinner.

Jesus recognises the woman's sin: 'But from now on do not sin again' (8:11). But the whole point of the passage is that he also raises the question of the sinfulness that is in all of those present: 'Let the one among you who is without sin, cast the first stone' (John 8:7). Sin is not just present in the woman who is the socially and religiously identified sinner but also in her accusers. And those of us reading that passage in the present are being asked to put ourselves into that scene. The passage asks us to see those identified as public sinners in our situation – whether this identification is explicit or implicit – as embodying something that is in all.

As we read that story, it asks us to place ourselves in the scene and to ask ourselves where we would stand: with the accusers? with the law? with those who gradually walked away? with rubbernecks who came to enjoy the 'fun' of a stoning? with the cynical bystanders? Or with Jesus?

There is this deeper sinfulness in human beings that the gospel calls us to be aware of and to attend to. It is within us and any acts or thoughts or omissions that we might see as sinful in ourselves or in others need to be related to this deeper reality of sinfulness or of 'the sin of the world'. This is brought to the surface by Jesus and it is taken on by him in his identifying it and in the event of his death in which he will be identified as the sinner. He will be in the place before his accusers that the woman was before hers.

This deeper sinfulness is not just the counting up of the sins of everyone but it is a power that lies within human beings and human societies that can find expression in people's attitudes and actions.

Evil – especially in its most fearful manifestations – is often described as an enigma, as something we cannot quite fathom, as something whose proper face we cannot see. This is the reason for the use of symbols in seeking to name it. And we can begin to see its true face when it comes into conflict with God and particularly with the presence of God in Jesus, the Holy One.

There is a certain similarity to the encounter between Jesus and human sinfulness in the encounters of Jesus with those who are afflicted with physical evils, even though sinfulness is not part of the scene in the latter encounters. Jesus treats such physical evils as being out of tune with the purposes of the creator; they are things that are not supposed to be there. We can find a vivid example of this in Mark's Gospel (1:23-28) where Jesus is confronted with physical evil identified with evil spirits. The unclean spirit cries out 'What do you want with us, Jesus of Nazareth? Have you come to destroy us? I know who you are: The Holy One of God'. That possessing 'spirit' is among the powers at work in our world that impede God's creative activity and that express the fact that the world is not as it should be.

Paul's sinfulness

In describing this deeper reality of sin, there is another New Testament passage that graphically highlights its reality. It is a passage that is constantly referred to in most Christian attempts to understand human sinfulness. It comes from Paul's Letter to the Romans in chapter seven, verses fourteen to twenty-three. It recounts Paul's own experience of sin. This passage reads:

> We know that the Law is spiritual: but I am of the flesh, sold as a slave to sin. I do not understand my own behaviour; I do not do what I want to do, but I do the thing that I hate. In the very act of doing what I do not want to do, I agree that the Law is good. So it is no longer myself acting but the sin that lives in me. For I know of nothing good living in me – in my flesh that is – for while it is open to me to want to do good, the power to do it is not; for the good thing I want to do, I do not do; the evil thing that I do not want – that is what I accomplish. But if I do what I do not want to do, then it is not myself acting, but the sin that lives in me. So I find this law for myself, that when I want to do good, evil opens up to me. In my innermost self, I delight in God's law, but I find another law in my body battling against the law of my mind and taking me prisoner to the law of sin that lives in my members. What a wretched man I am! Who will rescue me from this body doomed to death? Thanks be to God through Jesus Christ our Lord! So it is that with my mind I serve the law of God, but in my flesh I serve the law of sin.

This passage needs greater exegesis than is possible here. But in these words of Paul, Christians throughout the centuries have found a reflection of their own experience of the tension within themselves between goodness and sinfulness.

In this passage, Paul sees the law as that which shows what is good and what is evil. The law reveals what is sinful but – Paul suggests – the law leaves us at the mercy of sin. All the law can do is point it out. It does not have the power to enable us to be rid of the sin that it points out. Paul reflects on his own experience of being torn between good and evil. His experience is that sin lives within him and has power in him. Finally, he gives thanks to God who, in Jesus, delivers him from its power and sets him free.

All human beings live in the ambiguity described by Paul. We are in tension between the goodness within us and the power of sin that also has its voice and its power within us. Is this not something that we can all discover by reflecting on our own lives and selves? Even if only in small ways, the influence of sin is within us. Many people speak of the sinfulness they glimpse within themselves in the small acts and recurring attitudes that they find constantly coming up within them, despite the fact that they want to be rid of them.

One of the signs of the influence of Christ and his Spirit within us is that we can see – even in our small and constant faults – symptoms of that deeper reality of sin within us and what could perhaps happen were we to give ourselves over to it. Even more importantly, we can come to be able to laugh at this unwanted but recurring sinfulness in the knowledge that we are redeemed from it by Christ Jesus.

Sinner: symbol or scapegoat

The human behaviour seen at work in the story of the woman taken in adultery comes up several times in the

Gospels. It is something Jesus takes exception to in words and actions; he objects to the whole burden of sinfulness being loaded onto those legally portrayed as sinners.

We see this pattern of behaviour at work in the parable of the Pharisee and the publican. In this parable, it is made clear who goes home at rights with God: it is the publican who simply says 'Lord, be merciful to me a sinner', rather than the Pharisee who, in his self-righteousness, compares himself so favourably to the publican. Then there are those passages where the 'righteous' accuse Jesus of mixing with – and even worse – eating with those publicly identified as sinners (e.g. Matthew 9:9; Mark 2:13-14; Luke 5:29-32). The saying of Jesus about taking the plank out of our own eye before taking the speck out of the eye of others (Matthew 7:1-5), is aimed at this same pattern of behaviour.

And so the question: is the sinner symbol or scapegoat? Is the named sinner the only one in whom sin is to be found or is the sinner the symbol in whom we find something of ourselves reflected back to us?

The pattern of pointing out and pointing at the sinner occurs constantly in human affairs. The public sinner is pointed out as a wrongdoer – rightly perhaps – but what are the accompanying attitudes to this identifying of the sinner? Are they the same as those shown by the people surrounding the adulterous woman in the gospel? Or those of the Pharisee in the parable of the Pharisee and the publican?

Everyone is prone to the desire to distance themselves from responsibility for evil actions and the culpability involved. We want to show that we are not the culprit. We easily do what Adan and Eve do in the creation story as they refuse responsibility for their action, and so Adam scapegoats Eve and Eve scapegoats the snake.

This identification of others as sinners is grounded in a blindness that has caused much evil in human societies. A blindness that readily sees the speck in the other's eye while ignoring the plank in one's own. It is such self-righteousness that brings condemnation from Jesus as little else does. When we look back on the evil that is part of human history, blindness is clearly at work. It seems that such blindness can be unconscious but, on becoming conscious, it enters the realm of the intentional and deliberate.

Part of following Jesus is to see the seeds in our own selves of what can be seen in the one named as sinner. This does not obscure the evil perpetrated by the person who has done wrong but it does suggest that we see them in the light of our own potential to do wrong, our own capacity to give way to similar temptations.

A sinful Church

The Church especially needs the awareness of its own capacity for sinfulness to avoid the hypocrisy that Jesus so often condemns. *As part of its mission*, the Church needs a deep awareness of its own sinfulness.

Ambiguity is present in the Church as a body, as the People of God. The whole Church lives in this tension between goodness and sinfulness. This is not only how we are as believers but it *is how we are supposed to be!* We are the ambiguous People of God who believe in the Jesus who came to call sinners. We need to be always aware of the ambiguity within us. We need to acknowledge the Spirit who is at work in us just as we need to acknowledge the influence of sin within us. Every time the Christian community gathers for Mass, it acknowledges both the Spirit at work in it and the sinfulness that is also influential within it.

The Church is always in need of conversion. Everything that is human is in the Church because it is made up of human beings in whom there is a measure of everything that is in humanity, both of good and of ill. As believers in Jesus, Christians bring the human condition as it is into explicit contact and communion with him. This is the Christian condition; Christians live in that in-between state. They are as human as are all human beings, but are caught up into an explicit tension with Jesus Christ who reveals the world as God sees it, embodies God's forgiveness and opens up the path of union with God.

This ambiguity creates the saving tension called conversion. This conversion is the process by which human beings are being remade in the image of God who is their origin and end. It is a demanding process and it is only possible because, in Jesus, God has come into the midst of human beings. We are called to be refashioned in the image of the new man Jesus out of the distortion of the old man Adam, the image of humanity as it now is. A part of that distortion embedded in the old man is that of seeing ourselves as the righteous and seeing sin in others.

Christians are a people on the way to what they are intended to be. Their being on the path of conversion does not end until their pilgrim journey reaches its fulfilment in God's kingdom. And throughout that journey, they need symbols and rituals that keep their awareness of God's forgiveness and their own sinfulness before them.

The sexual abuse crisis has brought the sinfulness of the Church to the fore. It involves horrific evil. It should never have happened but along with other horrific things, it did happen. And there can be no absolute guarantee that incidents like it won't occur again. That creates the necessity of putting safeguards in place to protect against such occurrences. Why could it happen again? Because as said above, all that is in humanity is in the Church.

It is particularly horrific that this abuse occurred within the Church and that it was covered up by so many in authority within the Church. The Church has to repent of this evil, make recompense for it and become aware that it is itself a community of human beings in which evil is no stranger. The self-protection involved in the covering up of the incidents of sexual abuse is an instance of the Church unjustifiably protecting itself – an instance of self-centredness becoming a sinful closing upon itself at the expense of others who were made victims of that self-centeredness. This involved not just the acts of individuals but was part of the culture at work in the Church. It is an instance of social and structural sin.

The Church, the People of God, is a human reality whose very purpose requires that it acknowledge sinfulness at work within itself and in the world. It is called to name sin, repent of it and turn yet again to Christ who calls it beyond that sinfulness. A dulling of a sense of sin in the Church is to no one's advantage. But in order to avoid a deadening of the sense of sin, a new understanding of sin needs to come about.

The evil of idolatry was brought out into the light when it occurred within the people of the first covenant. That evil was at work in all the surrounding peoples who took it for granted but when it occurred in Israel it was dragged into the light and was revealed by the prophets as the diminishment of being human that it was. It was part of Israel's purpose to bring human sinfulness into the light so that it could be seen for what it was. In the case of the New Testament People of God, human evils ought to have their evil brought into the light of Christ's gospel, whether these occur outside the Church or within it.

Without the bringing of sin out into the light that occurs all along the development of the biblical tradition, sin could be seen as a natural and normal part of being human. It would be taken for granted as simply part of the way things are and are intended to be. Its power would be increased by its reduction to normality and inevitability. It is a part of the mission of the People of God to bring sin to the surface and to name it; but this has to be done in such a way that it can be recognised by contemporary people – even if they disagree with it.

Rites of Penance

It is important to integrate the question of the sinner as scapegoat or symbol into the celebration of rites of penance. In the first historical rite of penance in which the idolater, adulterer or murderer was excluded from the community, those identified as sinners were never actually fully excluded from the community but were differently part of it, which was specifically as penitents. They formed a group within the whole community. They remained within the community but, while penitents, could not participate in what lay at its heart – the Eucharist. Idolatry was probably the most frequent cause for the use of that rite and it had a unique place in the minds of those early Christians who lived in the insecurity of possible persecution. They knew that they could all be prone to the sin of denying the faith to save themselves. So the penitent idolater was a symbol for them all.

There are historical descriptions of the relationship of penitents to the rest of the community that express what they have in common and what is specific about the penitents. The penitents are described as prostrating and weeping while the rest of the community stood around them also weeping. The whole community participates in their journey in the knowledge of their common frailty as well as their common belonging to the same body of Christ.[40]

There were also practices that were part of the earliest recorded forms of individual penance in which there was a recognition on the part of the bishop or priest confessors of their own sinfulness before acting as confessors.[41]

---

[40] François Bussini, 'Intervention de l'assemblée des fidèles au moment de la réconciliation des pénitents d'après les trois 'postulationes' d'un archidiacre romain du Ve-VIe siècle', *Revue des Sciences religieuses* 41 (1967), 29-38.

[41] Mary C. Mansfield, *The Humiliation of Sinners: Public Penance in Thirteenth Century France.* Ithaca/London: Cornell University Press, 1995, 177-180; John Dallen, *The Reconciling Community.* NY : Pueblo Publishing Company, 1986, 113-119.

Chapter 8

Christ, Sin and the Sacrament of Penance

The death and resurrection of Jesus by which we pass-over from separation from God into communion with God presents us with the wonderfully mysterious ways of God. On encountering a world misshapen by sinfulness, the Christ does not take his distance from it or separate himself from it; nor does he take up arms against it, and, significantly, does not put an end to it. His way of dealing with it reveals to us the mystery of God present and at work in him who is God-among-us. He seems powerless before the evil he comes across; it has its way with him.

As we saw earlier on, the forces at work in Jesus' society that brought about his death prevailed over him. Such forces have had their way with countless human beings in the past and continue to do so in the present. Is God powerless before these forces? It could indeed seem so!

The story of Jesus is a very different story to the central story of the first testament – that of the Exodus, in which the enemy is defeated and destroyed. There are no enemies who die in the story of Jesus; the 'strong arm' of God does not appear. Embodied in Jesus and in his death and resurrection is a very different revelation of God. This new revelation had begun to be glimpsed and gradually sketched out by the prophets of Israel as we can see, for instance in Isaiah's figure of the Suffering Servant of God (Isaiah 42:1-9; 49:1-6; 50:4-11; 52:13 to 53:42).

Is God powerless before evil? As the very core of their faith, Christians keep celebrating Christ's victory over sin and death but that victory is far from obvious! It is only possible to name it and celebrate it as a victory in faith and hope. It can be nonsense to those who do not believe in Christ. It can be set aside as of no use to human beings just as Jesus Christ was set aside as being of no use to those who looked to him for what they thought a truly effective Messiah should be. In his death, he was set aside as of no importance perhaps even as a charlatan. To understand that Jesus Christ is God's response to evil and death requires a changed way of seeing things. It requires conversion, that is a going beyond human ways of seeing the world to let Christ's way of seeing things penetrate us.

The Christ who came among human beings does indeed confront us with the mystery of God, with a discovery of God beyond all the various meanings that that word can have in human minds and human cultures. There is revealed in Jesus the difference of God and the wonder of God. This God is discovered in the attitudes, the actions, and the death and resurrection of Jesus who is the One anointed by God to be his representative. In him, God is seen to be different to what human beings expect.

There are some words of a Belgian theologian, Adolph Gesche, that struck me when I first read them and have remained with me since: 'If God assumes suffering, it is because it is not explainable (otherwise he would have explained it), nor is it justifiable (otherwise he would have justified it), nor is it escapable (otherwise he would have escaped it – perhaps by some secret divine means), nor is it for the moment totally suppressible (or he would have done so). This is so because it can only be assumed and so be overcome'.[42]

This quotation shines light both on the enigma of evil and sin and on the mystery of God. We are redeemed from sin by this Jesus who is indeed one with us. We are redeemed by the Lamb of God who was afflicted by and takes away the power of the sin of the world to enclose humankind within it. He is the One who unburdens us from the power of this sinfulness by meeting it, allowing himself to be killed by it and in this strange and Godly way, he dealt with it.

The sacrament of penance that responds to the sinful dimension of human life is, therefore, a celebration of being redeemed by him who is the Lamb of God. And it does need to be a celebration of that redemption. Within the framework of redemption, all celebrations of reconciliation and penance need to be celebrated.

The formula of absolution currently in use in the Rite of Penance focuses in on the mystery of redemption: 'God the Father of mercies, through the death and resurrection of his Son, has reconciled the world to himself and has sent the

---

[42] Adolphe Gesché, *Pensées pour penser 1. Le Mal et la lumière*. Paris: Cerf, 2003, 37 (Author's translation).

Holy Spirit among us for the forgiveness of sins. Through the ministry of the Church, may God give you pardon and peace. And I absolve you from all your sins in the name of the Father, the Son and the Holy Spirit'.[43]

This formula epitomises the mystery that is being celebrated in the sacrament. It would be unfortunate to reduce this formula to the one earlier in use: 'I absolve you from all your sins in the name of the Father and of the Son and of the Holy Spirit'. Such a reduction would leave aside the richness of the mystery being celebrated in the sacrament, that is deliberately expressed in the renewed formula.

The sacrament of penance in any of its forms is a celebration of redemption. The legal model or even the healing model for the sacrament is not sufficient to reach into and express this fundamental Christian reality of redemption. We need to go to the heart of the mystery of redemption to grasp the meaning of this sacrament and the victory over sin which it celebrates. We are celebrating the Lamb of God who invades a humanity bent out of its true shape by sin, who takes to himself the sin of the world by allowing it have its way with him and who liberates human beings by means of a new power that he breathes into the world: the liberating, ennobling and divinising Spirit of God.

Any rite of penance needs to be celebrated, therefore, with its focus on Christ the Redeemer. What needs to be at

---

[43] *Rite of Penance*. (The Roman Ritual). Sydney, Wellington: E. J. Dwyer, 1975, nos 46, 55 and 62.

the forefront of any celebration is the fact that we are already redeemed, not just forgiven but redeemed, that is liberated from the *power* of sin. The Holy Spirit is already among us leading us out of sinfulness into union with Christ in whom we find the holiness of God.

We are already redeemed but sin still has its power in us. We are in the process of being redeemed: redemption is already at work in us, but so is sin. But in the process of redemption, we are freed from its *power*. We can step back from our sinfulness and distance ourselves from it because it has already been overcome by the power of Christ to whom we cling and whose Spirit is at work in us. The victory is already ours! ... But not yet!

In the sacrament of penance, the word absolution is used to speak of the act of reconciliation and forgiveness. The priest-celebrant does not say 'I forgive you your sins...' but 'I absolve you from your sins...'. He speaks of absolution because we are being loosed from the power of sin in us, we are being set free from it. Sinfulness is losing its power over us. This is forgiveness but a very particular kind of forgiveness; it is a loosening of our ties to sin by means a stronger interior tie to Christ. This expresses the paschal character of the sacrament, that is, we are passing over with Christ out of the power of sin into that union with the Father which Christ has brought into the world. Christ is the one who has invaded the house of the strong man and set us free (Matthew 12:29; Mark 3:27; Luke 11:21-22).

We cannot banish sinfulness from our lives, but we can name it and so draw it out into the light. In the biblical world, naming things was to have power over them. There is great wisdom in this: naming things, recognising the truth of our situation is a powerful step towards freedom from them.[44]

We do indeed need to be set free from the power of sin. Free from its power so that we may choose the good. For some people, this involves the need to be freed from ingrained sin or from seriously distorting sins. For others, it is the need to be freed from the fear of sin, while for others it may be the need to be freed from the impulse to think that they can be totally rid of sin's influence. And very importantly, for others, it may be the need for freedom from the image of a demanding even an implacable God that reinforces the power of sin in them.

Taking to heart the words of Paul in chapter seven of the Letter to the Romans in which he outlines his experience of sin, we need to take seriously the ending of the passage where we find Paul's exultant 'Thanks be to God through Jesus Christ our Lord'. Our celebrations of reconciliation and penance should reflect and help bring about such a cry of thanksgiving within us for the redemption we have received in Christ Jesus.

Celebrating redemption

From what has been said above, the celebration of reconciliation or penance is a celebration of the Paschal Mystery. In celebrating the Paschal Mystery of Christ's victory over sin

---

[44] We can also see this same power of naming things, of bringing them out into the light, in the work of psychologists who help people to recover the truth of a troubled situation.

121

and death, we celebrate the reality that we are forgiven sinners who are constantly being called to go beyond themselves in response to Christ's call to conversion.

Our approach needs to be centred on Christ and on our belonging to the Church his body, which is both sinful and holy. Some forms of such celebrations may be sacramental in the sense in which we are presently accustomed to use that word; others may be celebrations based on the general sacramentality of the Church as the basic sacrament of Christ. In patristic and early medieval times, the Church was more aware that all its celebrations and actions shared such sacramentality.[45] In its history, the Church has had a range of rites of penance and today we need to extend our range of celebrations again to achieve a healthier and richer understanding of forgiveness and sin.[46]

This general sacramentality of the Church finds expression in celebrations of the word of God and in the Church's communal prayer. This sacramentality is at work in the communal celebration of the Liturgy of the Hours,[47] as it is in such liturgies as the Installation of a Bishop, Religious Professions, and a variety of Consecrations and Blessings.

The theologian Peter Lombard (d. 1159), followed by the theologians of the twelfth and thirteenth centuries, limited

---

[45] See L-M. Chauvet, *Avances oecumeniques possibles en matière de sacrements.* Maison-Dieu 261 (2010), pp. 9-40. ; ibid., 'Sacrement: un concept analogique', in *Le Corps, chemin de Dieu. Les sacrements.* Paris: Bayard, 2010, pp. 35-53. (I have not been able to find this material in English so far).

[46] See Frank O'Loughlin, *op. cit.* esp. pp. 48-68.

[47] See 'The General Instruction on the Liturgy of the Hours', in *The Divine* Office. The Liturgy of the Hours according to the Roman Rite. Glasgow/Sydney/Dublin: Collins, E. .J. Dwyer, Talbot. 1974, no. 13.

the sacramental actions of the Church to the well-known list of seven rites. This listing became universal in the Church at that time because it was necessary to give a clear indication of what rites were constitutive of the Church's identity. So, for instance, the exclusion from the formal listing of the sacraments of such things as the anointing of kings and monastic profession – both of which were considered sacramental by some earlier theologians – made clear that those rites were not core rites of the Church and by doing so they clarified the very identity of the Church.

The listing of those seven rites indicated the centrality of those rites in the life and identity of the Church as the issues of the time required. An unfortunate consequence of this was to diminish the significance of all other rites of the Church, tending to dissociate them from God's giving of grace. We now need to recover that wider dimension of the Church's sacramentality in which any formally recognised action of the Church bears the significance of being an action of the Church as the body of Christ.

Further Rites of Penance

For the celebration of penance and reconciliation, the present Rite of Penance offers three rites that are considered strictly sacramental forms of penance. Other possible rites may be celebrated as suggested above as an action of the Church that is itself the sacrament of Christ. A basis for such further rites can be found in an appendix to the official rite of penance; it is presented under the title 'Sample

Penitential Services'.[48] At first glance, such celebrations can seem banal or ineffective but with further consideration and development, they can become effective means of celebrating redemption, the uncovering of sin and Christ's call to conversion.

The celebration of rites of penance cannot be ignored because the influence of sin is a reality in the life of the Church. Sin needs to be brought into the light. In the Church, as among all human beings, there is the capacity to turn a blind eye to sinfulness. Sin and God's response to sin have to find their place in the life of the Church so that sin is not allowed to hide its face.

The strong reaction among Christ's faithful to the use of confession as it was carried out in the earlier part of the twentieth century cannot be ignored. There are reasons for the fact that so many faithful and committed members of the Church simply do not use that form of the sacrament any longer. By and large, this means that they do not celebrate penance in any form. Their reasons need to be listened to.

In celebrating penance, I do not think that we should rush to the giving of absolution. We need to place emphasis on what comes before absolution and so enrich our understanding of sin, conversion, forgiveness and redemption. The use of such further celebrations can enable a deeper understanding and more effective practice. We need other rites that have value in themselves and that can also enrich the overall practice of penance and reconciliation in the life of the Church. Significantly, the first historical form

---

[48] *Rite of Penance*, op. cit. Appendix II, pp. 119-144.

of penance in the early centuries of the Church's life was focused on the identification of sin and on conversion. And we have something to learn from that in our present time.

It is also worth noting at this juncture that St Thomas Aquinas held that forgiveness was already brought about in the penitent by the very fact that they were contrite, that is that they had sorrow for their sin. When it came to speaking of the meaning of the priest's absolution, St Thomas spoke of a 'quondam ecclesiale', that is that it concerned the ecclesial dimension of the sacrament.[49] This ecclesial dimension is central to the sacrament. Penance is a sacrament of the Church; it is not therefore a purely individual matter. It expresses and recognises an element of the identity of the Church, that is that it is sinful and yet holy.

Like all sacraments, the sacrament of penance is a symbol of the Church. It expresses and effects a dimension of the Church's life that is core to its identity. And so even in an individual rite of penance, it is not just the penitent and the confessor who are involved but they are giving form to the Church as a holy but sinful reality.

This sacrament brings that ambiguous dimension of the Church's life to the fore and makes it concrete. The Church's innovation of a rite of penance after baptism in the first centuries of its life is part of the Church's gradual discovery of its own identity, a deeper and richer understanding and celebration of penance can bring about a similar discovery today.

---

[49] Frank O'Loughlin, *op. cit.* p. 75.

This ecclesial dimension of the sacrament is important because God's reconciling of human beings to himself is not just a matter of the individual. As God draws human beings to himself, he draws them to each other. In the resurrection, Christ raises up a body for himself that is the Church. Christ is himself risen but the community of the Church is his concrete means of embodiment in continuing history.

The concept of sin being put forward in this book in which the sins of the individual cannot be separated from the sinfulness of the world reinforces the ecclesial dimension of this sacrament. Human sinfulness is a communal reality, a part of human interconnectedness. The antidote offered by God is likewise communal. Christ is the new Adam embodying a new humanity; he gathers his frail disciples around him in his Church as a place where human sinfulness can be revealed in the light of his gospel. Human closeness to God is also a communal thing; it finds expression in the communion of saints.

By means of communal celebrations or a series of such – especially during Lent and Advent – we can come to appreciate more deeply the Christ who redeems us from sin, his call to conversion and the nature of our own sinfulness. Such celebrations need a specific celebration of the word, significant prayer and a ritual action that gives symbolic expression to their content and purpose. Such a ritual could be perhaps a laying on of hands, a renewal of baptismal promises, a rite based on the exorcisms of the *Rite of Christian Initiation for Adults* or an adapted form of the Penitential Rite used at Mass. There are models offered for such celebrations in the appendix at the end of this book.

Sin is not just an individual matter; it is part of us human beings who are socially formed, who live socially and who are caught up in and shaped by the social structures within which we cannot but live. We cannot understand sin – or celebrate it – by reducing it to individual actions or attitudes. Just as sin has individual, social and structural dimensions, so our celebrations need to have these same dimensions. We ought not to set aside any form of penance that we have at the moment but rather ought to enrich each of them and add others.

Chapter 9

How Much Does Sin Matter?

From a Christian point of view, an adequate understanding of and attitude to sin requires that we begin with the Christian belief in God's forgiveness of sin. God's forgiveness surrounds human sinfulness. Forgiveness is a gift which human beings have received from God through Jesus Christ. And as suggested earlier, we need to go further than speaking about forgiveness to speak about redemption. Redemption from both sin and death is given to us through the death and resurrection of Jesus Christ, the one who comes to us from God and who is the hand that God stretches out to sinners.[50]

This is truly a gift. It is received and cannot be earned (Romans 3:23-25a). It is a gift that prompts a response to God within the receiver, a response that begins with thanksgiving and goes on to reshape their lives.

And yet the reality of sin remains pervasive in our human world of which Christians are an integral part. It is present in small and individual ways and it is present in large scale ways that have terrible consequences. It is one of the forces that shape our world.

---

[50] See *Eucharistic Prayer II of Reconciliation*.

The redemption from sin which the gospel of Jesus Christ entails is a strange redemption. It is a redemption that will not force itself on human beings. We have a wonderful image of it in the Parable of the Prodigal Son which, as many have said, could well be called the Parable of the Prodigal Father. We find it in chapter fifteen verses eleven to thirty-two of the Gospel of Luke:

> Jesus said, 'There was a man who had two sons. The younger one said to his father, "Father, let me have the share of the estate that will come to me". So the father divided the property between them. A few days later, the younger son got together everything he had and left for a distant country where he squandered his money in loose living.
>
> When he had spent it all, that country experienced a severe famine, and now he began to be in need; so he hired himself out to one of the local inhabitants who sent him into the fields to feed the pigs. And he would willingly have filled himself with the pods which the pigs were eating, but no one would let him have them. Then he came to his senses and said, "How many of my father's hired men have all the food they want and more, and here am I dying of hunger! I will get up and go to my father and say: 'Father, I have sinned against heaven and against you; I no longer deserve to be called your son; treat me as one of your hired men'". So he got up and went back to his father.
>
> While he was still a long way off, his father saw him and was moved with pity. He ran to the boy, clasped him in his arms and kissed him. Then his son said, "Father, I have sinned against heaven and against you. I no longer deserve to be called your son". But the father said to his servants, "Quick! Bring out the best robe and put it on him; put a ring on his finger and sandals on his feet. Bring the fattened calf, and kill it; we will celebrate by having

a feast, because this son of mine was dead and has come back to life; he was lost and is found". And they began to celebrate.

Now the elder son was out in the fields, and on his way back, as he drew near the house, he heard music and dancing. Calling one of the servants he asked what it was all about. The servant told him, "your brother has come, and your father has killed the fattened calf because he has got him back safe and sound". He was angry then and refused to go in, and his father came out and began to plead with him; but he retorted to his father, "Look, all these years I have slaved for you and never disobeyed your orders, yet you never gave me so much as a young goat for me to celebrate with my friends. But, for this son of yours, when he comes back after swallowing up all your property with prostitutes you kill the fattened calf". Then the father said, "My son, you are with me always and all I have is yours. But it was only right we should celebrate and rejoice, because your brother here was dead and has come to life; he was lost and is found".

In this parable, the father does not stop the younger son from leaving him, from separating himself from him. Not only does he not stop him but he gives him 'whatever would be due' to him on his own (the father's) death! This act of the son is a radical cutting of his ties to the father, of his separating himself from his father. It is virtually the wish that his father was dead because that would normally be when he would receive 'what would come to him'. His going from the father is a deliberate act of separation from and disdain for the father. His action is egregious.

There is a parallel here between the younger son and the symbolic figures of Adam and Eve. In both cases, the protagonists are separating themselves from their source of life, their origin. The younger son shuns his dependence on the father, setting himself up as independent and without recognising his origin in the father. The Adam and Eve figures likewise give in to the temptation to separate themselves from God in order to become like gods themselves, so setting aside their origin and source of life in God.

The father in the parable gives the son freedom and gives it prodigally; he goes beyond the bounds of good sense!

This son wastes all that the father has given him and ends up destitute and working with pigs! He has reduced himself to that state ultimately by his decision to separate himself from the father.

And yet somewhere within him, the memory and influence of the father remains real. In his desperate circumstances, the thought of the father comes to his mind and he somehow knows that he can return to the father in his state of desperation. He does not expect to be re-instated as son but he knows he would be better off even as a hired hand on his father's property. 'So he got up and went back to his father' (v. 20).

His motivation may not be all that pure. It is his desperation that drives him home. Perhaps he even had certain calculating thoughts.

The father sees him coming home while he is still at a distance: 'When he was still a long way off, the father saw him... he ran to the boy, clasped him in his arms and kissed him' (vv. 20-21). It is as if the father has been hanging over the gate scanning the horizon for this lost son!

The son puts forward his proposal that he is no longer worthy to be the father's son but should be only a hired man. But with this father such cannot be the case. The best robe is brought out, a ring is put on his finger and sandals on his feet, the fattened calf is killed and a feast is declared because 'this son of mine was dead and has come back to life; he was lost and is found' (v.22-24). There is no question of half measures with this father. This young man is son again!

This is not just forgiveness, it is redemption. The son is set free from all he has done, even from his implied wish that the father was dead. He is restored to his sonship; bounty is poured out upon him.

In writing the above, I have been constantly tempted to spell 'father' as 'Father', so closely and deliberately does the image of the father in this parable reflect God our Father, the One whom our Lord Jesus Christ calls 'Abba, Father'. This parable gives us this graphic image of the Father of whom Jesus speaks. In it we see imaged the God of untiring love and endless goodness.

But then there is the elder son! It is easy enough for us to feel sympathy for him. He has done the right thing! But he is mean and ungracious to his brother in contrast to the father. Would he have liked to have done what the younger son had done? Or is he just self-righteous? His heart is not that of the father. His heart is set upon his own self and his rights. At the end of the parable, it is he who is separating himself from his brother and from his father! Is his self-righteousness and meanness such that he cannot be at one with the father whose heart is so different? Is this son an image of those people Jesus comes across in the gospels whose self-righteousness and condemnation of others so angered him?

We are dealing with this God who is imaged in the prodigal father and who is beyond us in so many ways. Our very capacity to sympathise with the elder son should alert us to a capacity within us to centre ourselves upon ourselves and thus to close ourselves off from God and each other. The Father revealed by Jesus cannot be made to back up our very human judgments; he cannot be constrained or limited by human standards.

Along with the above parable, there are two other small parables in the same chapter fifteen of Luke's Gospel: that of the lost sheep and that of the lost coin (vv. 4-10). They both give the same image of God in different ways: the image of a God who loves beyond reason. In the first, the ninety-nine sheep are left at risk to go after the one who is lost; and in the other the woman exerts such effort to find the one lost coin of her ten.

We find this same sort of image of God in Matthew's Gospel in the words: 'But I say this to you, love your enemies and pray for those who persecute you; so that you may be children of your Father in heaven, for he causes his sun to rise on the evil as well as the good, and sends down rain on the righteous and the wicked alike' (5:45, see also Luke 627-36).

We are redeemed by the love that God has for us that is made manifest in Christ Jesus our Lord (Romans 8:37-39). This is forgiveness beyond forgiveness; it is the restoration of all our human dignity as those made in the image of God.

This parable is, however, quite unfinished. The story remains unresolved at the end. What does the elder son end up doing? And the younger son? And the father? What happens? Do we have an instance of one of those constant alienations that are so much part of human life? Will this whole story be one of continuing separation? Do we have the potential for a repetition of the ancient story of Cain and Abel – one of the great scriptural images of human sinfulness? Or will the love of the father/Father win out?

The overwhelming nature of God's love does not mean that we can do whatever we like. The incompleteness of this parable sets up the need for a response from everyone who reads it. What happens from thereon in? God never takes our freedom from us. He will never diminish us but sets a task before us, opening us up to the call to go beyond ourselves and to let his love find a means of coming into our world in and through us.

All of us are called to complete this parable in our own lives and relationships. And we can only do that by coming close to the Father and letting his Spirit begin to penetrate and possess us.

Human beings are redeemed. And we who are of the Church are the witnesses to this redemption. We have received this revelation of God's love through Jesus Christ but it is a gift for all humankind, our sisters and brothers. We are indeed called to be sisters and brothers to all humankind.

Our redemption is a strange redemption. It does not bring about the disappearance of sin from our world. God's mysterious ways never destroy, but respect the freedom of the human beings he has created in his image. God is always like the father of the prodigal son who lets the son go off with his inheritance even if it means that this separation from himself will be to his detriment.

What is recounted in the gospels is for us now! It is not so much about what happened back then in the time of Jesus but about what is now and always going on between ourselves and God through Jesus. Those stories, words and events reveal not only what was going on then between Jesus and his contemporaries but about what God is now seeking to bring about between himself and human beings through Jesus. We are intended to read ourselves into those gospel narratives every time we hear them or read them.

We live in memory of those events. We live with them as our guides into the mystery of life. We use them to interpret ourselves, our interactions with others and with God. What Christ did and said back then, he continues to do and say with new impact in our different time and context.

Another image of the redemption we have received is given us in the Lord's Prayer. In the translation most in use, we pray, 'Forgive us our trespasses as we forgive those who trespass against us' but the better translation is 'Forgive us our debts...'. This is an image of God's forgiveness in terms of the cancelling of debts. God does not alter the interest rates on our debts; he forgives or cancels the debt itself. Imagine the response of joy within anyone whose debt is simply wiped away, not altered or diminished but removed. Such is the image of God's forgiveness given to us in the Lord's Prayer. In Jesus, God himself redeems our debts.

The forgiveness of sin is no commercial transaction; it does not involve bargaining. Forgiveness and redemption are poured out upon us and seek to set us up as a means by which God's compassionate love can flow into human affairs, that is 'as we forgive those who are in debt to us'. This is a gift given to create more giving in the receivers. It is all God's work. The father in the above parable does not let the son bargain; he cuts him off before he gets to his planned words about being a hired man. The son has his bargain all worked out beforehand, but it is swept away by the father's abounding love.

Already but not yet

We are redeemed already but we are not yet redeemed! This phrase sums up a fundamental aspect of the Christian life. We are already at home with God. We have already been clothed in the best robes and have had a ring put on our fingers and have had a feast laid for us. The love and forgiveness of God has already been poured out over all of humankind! Christians are called to be the witnesses to that love and forgiveness.

But we are not yet redeemed! It is more than clear that involvement in evil is still part of being human in small and great ways and that our redemption is far from complete.

What we have now is a deposit on the future yet to come. We live in the sure and certain hope that God will complete what he has begun. We are a people of hope and that hope rests on the fidelity of God who, in the death of Jesus, has shown that he will stop at nothing to bring his world to himself.

God's work of continuing to redeem human beings takes place by means of the Holy Spirit who is at work in all the world. The activity of the Spirit never ceases and will never cease. The Spirit is the Spirit of Christ who works away constantly to give effect to the 'new and eternal covenant' made by God with all humanity in the death and resurrection of Jesus.

This word 'covenant', as we saw earlier, means a relationship or an alliance. This word describes a new relationship being offered by God to human beings in and through Jesus. God is in an alliance with us in our human existence. This relationship – which is imaged in the Scriptures as a marriage – will never be abandoned by God. 'Divorcing' human beings will never be part of God's purposes.

This new relationship will never cease being offered by the Holy Spirit to human beings in all their affairs. The Spirit will never cease being operative in every dimension of humanity's life. Wherever the Beatitudes are being lived, there the Spirit of Christ is at work, because that Spirit is also the Breath breathing through all of creation, keeping it alive. This Spirit is not an idea or an ideal or an inspiration; but is that quiet person of the Trinity at work in all of creation and in a uniquely self-revealing way among the followers of Jesus Christ.

The Spirit is the quiet unnamed one who in the heart of the younger son of the parable – despite the ambivalence of his motives – raises up his awareness that he can go back to the father. We believers are witnesses to the presence and activity of the Spirit whom we can name because Jesus has revealed him to us.

At this point, I would like to quote again the preface of the Second Eucharistic Prayer of Reconciliation that speaks so well of the Spirit of God at work in our world:

> In the midst of conflict and division, we know it is you who turn our minds to thoughts of peace. Your Spirit changes our hearts: enemies begin to speak to one another, those estranged join hands in friendship, and nations seek the way of peace together. Your Spirit is at work when understanding puts an end to strife, when hatred is quenched by mercy, and vengeance gives way to forgiveness.

Those who make up the Church live out explicitly this tension between what is already and what is yet to come. They are always in a state of conversion, of being called beyond ourselves. There is always a tension between sinfulness and goodness. This tension is not accidental; it is an essential part of the life of the Church and of the individual Christian. Awareness of this tension is necessary if we are to understand our own identity and mission.

The need for this awareness is one of the reasons that we require celebrations of reconciliation/penance. It is not a good thing to fail to acknowledge our need for redemption and for the conversion consequent to it.

It is also a failure in understanding sin if we so speak about it that it seems more powerful than God's forgiveness and redemption. Our celebrations need to be more effectively celebrations of redemption and of the call to conversion.

Another significant aspect of the Christian life as caught in the 'already but not yet' tension is that it redescribes the relationship between the life we live now and the life to which we look forward in the future. Our life now is not merely a preparation for the life to come much less a testing ground to see if we are worthy of it. Rather, human life now can offer an opening for that future to be seeded into the present; or – to put it another way – for the kingdom of God to continue coming into our world. In going beyond ourselves and opening ourselves up to the ways of God, we are letting something of God's kingdom come in among human beings. This is true of believers but also of all human beings in whom the Spirit of God is at work.

So we see a life in tune with the gospel of Christ as anticipating the life to come. In the Lord's Prayer, we pray: 'May your will be done on earth as it is in heaven'. We pray that the future will come into the present. We pray that things will come about on earth as they do in heaven.

Continuing sinfulness

During a homily, I once remember saying that I could sometimes see the seeds of Hitler in myself in response to which some parishioners suggested that they had better keep an eye on me!

One of the genuine elements of Christian experience is that there is a sinfulness that continues within us even despite us! This is a crucial point in understanding sinfulness. Many sensible people talk about the fact that despite many resolutions to be rid of sinful attitudes, such attitudes remain within them. Such attitudes may be a matter of being judgmental, of anger, of envy, of desire, of seeing everything in a self-centred way, or of wanting to be rid of people who impede our way ahead. Some selection of such feelings is within us all. What is even more interesting is that so often such feelings arise within us *before we are aware of them*; we notice them only after they have arisen within us.

This brings up a capital point in understanding one aspect of human sinfulness. It is there within us before we notice it. Such feelings and attitudes are not going to disappear: they are part of us. They witness to the 'sin of the world' that in some way is in all of us. It is something all human beings share. These feelings and attitudes should not be considered as personal sin but as part of our belonging to humankind in its present situation. This is a sinfulness that we have not personally brought about but that somehow has been brought about in us. This is part of what we have seen in the symbolic description of the interplay between Adam, Eve and the snake. It is a part of us that we need to learn to recognise and entrust into God's hands.

Earlier, I spoke of laughing at our sinfulness. This is the right approach to this continuing sinfulness that we find within ourselves. It is this sinfulness that we share with all humankind and from which we have been redeemed. Our response ought to be that we do not let it cause us to feel separated from God, but rather that we bring it out into the light of our relationship with God and entrust it – along with everything else – into his hands. We can laugh at it because we have been redeemed from it, even though it still persists! It is a snake whose real venom has been removed from it.

The problem of personal sin only arises when we take up these feelings and attitudes and turn them into deliberate attitudes and act on them. In doing that, we are adding to the sinfulness of the world and in refraining from it, we are lessening of the sinfulness of the world.

An attitude to this continuing sinfulness that treats it as something completely within our control can result in giving up on ourselves or on following Christ. And it can lead to the suffering of scrupulosity. Such scrupulosity tends to arise from a combination of a legalist approach, a defective image of God and particular types of personality difficulty. Scrupulosity can turn people's relationship to God into something torturous in that they feel that they can never be free of sin and so cannot be pleasing to God. Such an understanding re-enforces the power of sin.

On the other hand, many people have made common sense decisions that such sinfulness as simply being part of the human race and deal with 'sensibly'. This is also a reason for the present very significant drop off in the use of traditional confession in so many parts of the church. That practice could at times seem like killing gnats with hammers!

And, of course, perfection is not a human possibility in the life we are all now living. This is a point made in the canonisation of saints. Often, in the past, the saints were presented as if they were perfect, but in reality we are being presented with people who were holy, that is close to God despite the human imperfection that was part of them.

The fact that perfection cannot be achieved in this world warns us against idealists who aim to bring about what they see as a perfect world. As history shows us, such attitudes so often turn to violence to achieve their end.

The human psyche is wounded, and in some cases seriously so. This wounded-ness always needs to be taken into account in dealing with human sinfulness – and human holiness. And often people are in need of professional psychological help if they are to be free from what they see as their 'sinfulness'. We cannot ignore the fact that what is termed 'sin' may indeed be a wounded-ness that impedes not only the person's subjective capacity to sin, but their capacity to understand their life sensibly and to live it contentedly.

Daily sins

Among the Fathers of the Church and in the first historical rite of penance, serious sins were those that threatened one's existence as a Christian, that is one's being a disciple of Christ. As we have already seen, such sins were identified as idolatry, adultery and murder.

On the other hand, what the Fathers of the Church called 'daily sins' were seen as forgiven by one's ordinary participation in the life of the Church and in the traditional trio of almsgiving, fasting and prayer. In evaluating our understanding of sin and the ways it is dealt with, we need to take into account such practices of the ancient Church.

Along that same line of thinking, St Augustine suggests that every time we pray the Lord's Prayer, we are loosed from such daily sins, because in that prayer we re-orient ourselves towards God.[51] We have such practices or their equivalents in the life of the Church today, especially the Mass and the seasons of Advent and Lent.

Celebrating Mass

That re-orientation of which St Augustine speaks occurs in the Liturgy of the Mass. This is the supreme prayer of God's people, and is the action in which the People of God express and rediscover who they are. Every time the members of the Christian community gather for Mass, they acknowledge their sinfulness and entrust themselves to the loving mercy of God, who in the delightful phrase of Isaiah 38:17, 'throws their sins behind his back'. And every time they celebrate Mass, they engage again in that 'wonderful exchange' in which they give over their lives to God in and through Christ and they receive the seeds of that new life of freedom from sin and death that comes with the Eucharistic sharing in the life of the resurrection.[52]

During Mass the People of God not only pray the Penitential Rite at its beginning, but they pray often in

---

[51] See Augustine's Sermon 213 which can be found in L. J. Johnson, *Worship in the Early Church Vol 3*, Adelaide: ATF Press, 2009, 64. There is a useful summary account of Augustine's position in James Dallen, *The Reconciling Community. The Rite of Penance.* NY: Pueblo Publishing Company, 1986, pp. 60-1.

[52] See Brian P. Flanagan, *Stumbling in Holiness. Sin and sanctity in the Church*, pp. 26ff.

the psalms to the One who, as Psalm 86 says, is 'is compassionate and gracious, slow to anger, abundant in mercy and fidelity'.[53] Also the readings of the Mass often deal with human sinfulness and God's forgiveness. And the liturgy frequently calls upon the Christ, who is the Lamb who takes away the sin of the world.

The Penitential Rite is a major moment of concentration on sin and forgiveness within the celebration of the Mass. The three forms of this rite as given in the Missal are significantly different and ought to be chosen in accord with their suitability for each particular celebration. Each of these forms has the structure of an introductory formula said by the priest followed by a pause for silence, then there follows the body of the prayer and a formula of absolution said by the priest.

It is notable that the Missal calls those final words of the priest an absolution without intending to equate it to the absolution that forms part of the sacrament of penance. It is, however, referred to as an absolution; it is an example of a broader sense of the availability of forgiveness within the practice of the Church than has been the case in recent centuries. It tallies with the practice of the ancient Church mentioned above.

The body of the penitential rite in each form is different. The first form is taken from the traditional prayer called the *Confiteor* and emphasises the community's and each individual's acknowledgment of their sin.

---

53 Psalm 86:15-16; 103:8-18; 145:8.

In the second form, the prayer takes the form of a very short and simple dialogue between the priest and the people: 'Have mercy on us, O Lord. For we have sinned against you. Show us, O Lord, your mercy. And grant us your salvation.' Its brevity can be suitable for particular occasions.

The third form is made up of three phrases followed by 'Lord, have mercy' or 'Christ, have mercy' that the people repeat after the priest. In this form, the phrases acclaim Christ as Saviour and so the emphasis is on what the Lord has done for his people rather than their sinfulness. These phrases can be chosen in accord with the feast or the readings of the day. Apart from the formulae given in the Order of Mass, there are other sample formulae given in Appendix VI of the Missal. It is to be noted that these are described as samples and so do not exclude the choice of other possible formulae. They are there as models for further local adaptation.

The other ritual within the Mass that is particularly relevant to our topic is the Sign of Peace. This is a sign that seeks to bring out our unity over against the separation that can so bedevil human and Christian communities. The Sign of Peace is about unity and because of that it is also about reconciliation, about overcoming those tendencies to dispersion that are strong within humankind as they are among the followers of Christ.

The sign of peace is not a sign of friendship but a sign of a unity that goes beyond friendship as friendship is dependent on our human likes and dislikes. It is about a unity and a reconciliation that God seeks to create in the People of God by drawing them to the one table to share the one bread whoever they are and whatever their human condition. Were someone to be seated beside another person at Mass whom they thought of as an enemy, it would bring out forcefully the ultimate point of the sign of peace.

Lent and Advent

The People of God pay special attention to redemption, conversion and sin each year in the course Lent – the season that leads into the Easter celebration of redemption. The Sunday and weekday readings and prayers of Lent are a treasure trove of inspiration for the following of Christ in all its aspects.

The three traditional activities of Lent are prayer, fasting and almsgiving. Each of these is a means of going beyond ourselves, that is of counteracting our self-centredness and taking us beyond self-interest in response to Christ's call to conversion. In prayer, we go beyond ourselves by giving over time to God thus creating space for God and his word in our lives. By fasting, we seek to loosen the hold that our own desires have on us and so to increase our freedom from them. In almsgiving or the giving away of our goods, we loosen the hold that possessions can have on us. Each of these activities take us beyond ourselves and enable us to enter into fuller communion with God and other people.

Advent is another time that gels with our purposes here. Advent is not so much about personal conversion as is the case with Lent; it is rather an invitation to look at the world around us and to see that it is not in a satisfactory state. Our human world is not as it should be. There is something wrong with it. Advent urges us to see that the world as we know it is not as God desires his world to be. And so it is a time for shining some light on 'the sin of the world'.

This season moves towards Christmas, the feast of the coming of Christ into our world, the feast of his Incarnation. He not only has compassion for our world and pours out his forgiveness upon it but he becomes part of it, so much a part of it that anything that can happen to us, could have happened to him! He enters our world to assure its future in God.

So it is that in Advent we call on him to keep coming, to keep identifying with us and our world. We call on him to keep on being Emmanuel (God-with-us) in the midst of this imperfect and disturbed world that is clearly not as it should be.

The People of God are constantly engaged in the celebration of Mass and the celebration of liturgical seasons by which they are being loosed from their ordinary daily sinfulness by entering anew into communion with God and each other.

The sin of the world

This phrase from the Gospel of John (1:29, 31) appears in the Liturgy of the Mass six times: twice during the Gloria, three times during the Lamb of God and once at the Invitation to Communion. And as noted earlier, in the first chapter of the Gospel of John, the word 'sin' is in the singular not the plural.

The use of this phrase enables us to touch on that deeper reality of sin that has been a crucial thread in the understanding of sin set forth in this book. It is this sin of the world – that is the sinful condition of humankind – that Christ the Lamb of God takes away. He frees humankind from it. It is no longer the determining force in the shaping of the human future that it had the potential to be. There is always another force at work seeking to impede its ultimate consequences that is the Spirit of the risen Christ. Just as death has been robbed of its ultimate power by Christ so has sin because God – from whom sin separates us – is now with us in this radically new way.

Whatever sins human beings commit, we need to see them as related to this deeper reality of the sin of the world. Sins are the means by which this deeper reality can show its face. Serious personal sin can increase the sin of the world by affirming and promoting it. Just as human attitudes and actions that go beyond self-centredness diminish its influence in humankind.

To 'hand oneself over to sin' is to align oneself with this sinfulness and become one with it. In such a case, it shapes the person's life and has evil consequences for the lives of others. We can see such sinfulness in those instances of human involvement in evil that have become paradigms of evil.

'Handing oneself over to sin' is an utterly different matter to any other instance of sin; it is allowing oneself to be taken over by sin. Serious sin can indeed be just that for the perpetrator and other people affected by it; but the sinner can also take their distance from their sin regretting it and seeking to repair the damage caused by it. What have traditionally been called venial sins are slips up along the way that do not change the orientation of one's life.

Social and structural sin refer to that sinfulness that is not just built into human beings as individuals but is part of them as social beings who live in social structures. Social attitudes and social structures determine the way human beings act and embody the values of their societies. So the structures of a society can be so weighted towards the rich that justice to the poor is unachievable, or they can be so weighted towards individual freedom that the communal dimension of being human is undermined. Social attitudes and structures can be such that the lives of some people are valued above those of others: such as when women are seen as of less value than men, or black people of less value than white people, or people of different sexual orientations seen as ipso facto evil. People can be regarded as traitors because they are revealing a truth about the society or group they live in; such whistle-blowers can thus be seen as pariahs because they reveal a truth that is unpalatable to the accepted mentality or mores of the group. People with renewing ideas can be seen as unfaithful to their culture or tradition on no other grounds but that they are inviting others to see things differently.

Such things occur because of the attitude of the whole social body and its ethos which experiences threat in what is new or different. Such structures act like a mental prison not only for those who seek to change them but for those enclosed within them.

Sin and punishment

This may be the right place to deal with a topic that has always been part of the understanding of sin and that is punishment for sin.

In the legal understanding of sin, the punishment for sin was seen as imposed by God acting as a judge who rewards or punishes in accord with the person's conduct. Looking at sin as proposed in this book, the relationship of sin and punishment is quite different.

Sin brings its own punishment with it. If people were to really give themselves over to sin, that behaviour shapes them. They set in train a process by which they cut themselves off from God who is the fountain of life and the one in whose image they have been made. In so doing they also cut themselves off from others. This applies to the extreme instance of sin, that of handing oneself over to it, or making it the deliberate and defining element of a personal way of life.

The extreme of this extreme is the sin against the Holy Spirit (Matthew 12:31-32; Luke 12:10), in which no room is left for the Holy Spirit to act. It is sin that excludes the Spirit's redeeming presence in human affairs.

It is in this situation that the notion of Hell enters. Hell is the ultimate closure to God. God does not withdraw from human beings but it seems that human beings can withdraw from God. Hell is the ultimate cutting of the tie to the fountain of life. In so doing would not that person be moving toward the extinction of their life? This is what is sometimes called the second death in the Scriptures (Revelation 20:6, 14; 21:8). Images of Hell in the past were often images of destruction especially that of fire or in some medieval art the image of being eaten by Satan, the figure of evil, and then being turned into his excrement.[54]

Purgatory in the legal model is a temporary place or state of punishment.[55] Like Hell it was usually, but not always, associated with fire. Such imagery was too often taken literally. Purgatory is rather the completion of our conversion, that same conversion that we are undergoing in our present lives. It is coming to be fully our true selves in the encounter with the One in whose image we are made. Such an encounter involves the purifying of all that stands between us and our Creator. This is the continuation of the encounter with the Lord that is part of our lives now.

Before there was any formal talk of Purgatory in the Christian tradition,[56] there was the image of a journey to God to be completed in the dying of the Christian. It was for this reason that processions are still a significant element in the Christian funeral service. The procession was not only practical but symbolic. The procession is an image the journey of the person to God. The community of faith accompanies the deceased on this journey in a procession

---

[54] For example, images from Albi Cathedral and the Scrovegni Chapel in Padua.

[55] *Catechism for General Use in Australia*, op. cit. p. 23, question 97.

[56] See Jacques Le Goff, *The Birth of Purgatory*. Chicago: University of Chicago Press.1984.

of solidarity and prayer. The journey to God was the way in which the need for the completion of the Christian journey of conversion was imaged. Pilgrimage was also seen in the light of this journey.

These processions give expression to the lovely reality that the Christian community is a community also in the passing over to God of one of its members. That deceased member remains part of the communion of saints. These processions express the communion of saints spread out over heaven and earth and the journeying in-between.

This same communion between the living and the dead is the reason why the Eucharist is also central to the Christian funeral. The Eucharist is the supreme expression of the communion of the faithful with God in this present life. This communion is enjoyed in its fullness by those who have gone before us.

Celebrations of reconciliation/redemption

It was mentioned earlier on that, in 1973, following the Second Vatican Council the new Rite of Penance was published, in which there were three sacramental Rites of Penance and an appendix entitled 'Sample Penitential Services'. The 1973 document was a significant step forward but, as with any document, it is a product of its time and the time preceding it.

The first rite of individual confession and absolution has its roots in the Middle Ages. It was originally a more protracted rite in terms of its ability to enhance the penitent's journey of conversion. In our current situation, this rite needs considerable development including an explicit and required use of the Scriptures, an emphasis on the penitent's self-discovery and their journey of conversion. Because of a greatly increased number of people wishing to use the sacrament during the twentieth century in particular, there was pressure to make the rite as short as possible. There were also those who used the sacrament as part of their spiritual journey and as a form of spiritual direction.

The second rite involves a communal celebration that includes individual confession and absolution as either part of the rite or at its end. This rite can be effective for smaller groups of people with a sufficient availability of confessors to make it practicable.

The third rite involves a silent, general confession of sins followed by general absolution. This has traditionally been used in extraordinary circumstances such as its use with soldiers in war time. There was some use of this rite in the years after its publication in 'The Rite of Penance' but its use became more and more restricted by Church authorities.

However, maybe the time has come to reconsider the use of this rite especially in the light of a different way of thinking about sin. Its communal character is valuable in this regard. However, I would put two riders on the use of this form of the sacrament. First, I believe that what needs to emphasised in the reform of this sacrament is the process of conversion, rather than an overemphasis on absolution.

And secondly, when this rite was in use, there was a rider attached to it which was that people who had sinned seriously needed to confess their sin to a priest after the celebration of the third rite. This all depends, of course, on what is meant by serious sin. But there is a point to this rider that is important. When dealing with a sinfulness that has a grip on the penitent, more than a quick absolution is necessary. That person needs appropriate personal help in dealing with such sin. It is also noteworthy that the rider does not say that the person has to receive absolution again but to make a confession of their sins.

I come back to a point I have made earlier on and that is that we need celebrations of penance/reconciliation/redemption that tease out this dimension of the Christian life. We need celebrations that are centred on the redemption Christ has brought to us, on his call to conversion and on bringing sinfulness into the light.

However much sin matters, redemption matters more. Redemption is more than forgiveness; it is more than reconciliation. The story of the Prodigal Son with which we began this chapter is not just about the forgiveness of the Father or the son's reconciliation with him. It is about the Father who hangs over the gate looking and longing for the son's return. It is about the lavish reception that the son receives from this insanely loving Father. The son is redeemed: he is clothed in the best robe, a ring is put on his finger and sandals on his feet and a feast is set for him. He is redeemed; he is set free from his past and enters an unlooked-for future of being a son as he has never been a son before. Grace is poured out upon him.

And all of this sets a new path before him. How will he relate to the father? How will he relate to the older brother? How will he live within his father's house and domain?

Conclusion

So does sin matter? Yes, it does. It is indeed a force to be reckoned with in human life; it has power in the working of human societies and in each person's life. Its presence in human history is glaringly obvious. Human beings make decisions for and against it. But it is not something which is simply within the control of human beings and their decisions; it is not just a matter of good choices and bad choices. It is a power with us individually and socially and it is embodied in the social structuring of human societies. The snake of the Adam and Eve story is a great symbol of it. It is there in the undergrowth slivering around, so to speak. It incites men and women to accede to its temptations.

And so it is that we return to a point made often in this book – we cannot simply reduce sin to the sinful acts of human beings. Such acts may express it and even reinforce it but to reduce sin to such acts is to ignore its real power and influence. And to reduce sin to the peccadillos that Catholics have often confessed in the sacrament of penance without seeing them in the relation to this deeper sinfulness is to trivialise this very real dimension of human existence.

Human beings are being redeemed from this sin even though it still has power within them. Attitudes to sin need to be shaped by a concentration on Christ the Redeemer who enables us to stand back in freedom from the sinfulness that is within us because he has made of it a de-venomed snake, so long as we do not go along with its power within us.

We need to keep bringing sinfulness out into the light; to bring all of its aspects – personal, social and structural – out into the light of God's word. By doing this, we face up to it and acknowledge its power within us by naming it. In so doing, we can keep removing its venom. Over against the influence of sin in the world, we constantly go to Christ to entrust ourselves and our sinfulness into his redeeming hands. And again – as said above – there are multiple ways in which we can do this – all of which are valuable. There is a need to develop more deeply our understanding of Christ's redemption along with our own sinfulness and need for conversion. In responding to this need, I would suggest that the use of celebrations of redemption and reconciliation such as suggested in the Appendix of this book would be helpful and enriching.

Living in an age that is radically an age of transition, the understanding and practice of Christian faith is also in transition. Living in such ages is always a matter of continuity with the past and difference to the past.

Our understanding of sin will not be immune from this transition. Such has been the case in earlier times of transition and will be the case today. Hopefully, this book has helped to lay some foundations for this transition in our understanding of sin and our ecclesial ways of dealing with it.

The fundamental scriptural understanding of sin as separation from God is crucial to this. And, biblically, that separation from God is the root from which our separation from each other grows. Separation is, in a way, a tame word; but it is fundamental. Our history shows what evils can grow in the fertile soil created by that separation.

'Christ yesterday and today, the Beginning and the End, the Alpha and the Omega. All time belongs to him and all the ages. To him be glory and power through every age and for ever.' This is proclaimed at the Easter Vigil as the Easter Candle is marked out to be a symbol of the Risen Christ. But this symbol is also marked with the signs of his death as five studs filled with incense are inserted into the candle. These represent the five wounds of Christ.

The Risen One bears the marks of his suffering and death, that death imposed on him by human beings in their slavery to a distorted condition that makes them blind. And as we have seen, those present at his historical death were symbolic of what occurs throughout human history. But words are said by the Lord Jesus that are like balm poured out over troubled humanity: 'Father, forgive them; they do not know what they are doing'.

And as he is risen out of death and the power of the sin that brought about his death, so are we being brought out of the power of death and sin into the new life of his resurrection. His Spirit is always at work seeking to bring about this new way of being human.

Appendix

Celebrations of Redemption/Reconciliation

The following celebrations are offered as models for communal celebrations of redemption/reconciliation within the Church's overall practice of penance and reconciliation. Such celebrations as these have been suggested more than once within the text of this book. Note that the celebrations may be directed by a priest, deacon or lay leader.

The use of the word 'redemption' is deliberate as that aspect of the Christian Faith has not been sufficiently brought to the fore in the celebration of rites of penance or, as far as I know, in writings about them. Redemption is a gift of God to human beings that has been hard won by Christ our Saviour through his death and resurrection. I would hope that these celebrations can help to draw out a greater richness of faith in Christ and so to deepen our appreciation of the Mystery of Faith.

Penitential Services can be rather banal. It is for this reason that I have suggested that further reflections and prayer forms be included along with symbolic actions towards which the celebrations move. These symbolic actions seek to embody what has also been celebrated in the word of God and in prayer in the course of each celebration.

All of these actions are derived from various rites that are already used in the Church's liturgical practice.

Silence plays a part in each of these celebrations. It is an element of our liturgy that is too often neglected. One of the rhythms that is important for the fruitfulness of the liturgy is the interplay between its communal character and the personal, spiritual participation of each member of the gathered community. Silence is important in enabling this. Communal prayer and personal prayer feed into each other.

CELEBRATION 1
'The Lamb of God who takes away the sins of world'

Notes for the Celebration

1. The suggested focus for the celebration is the principal crucifix of the church.

2. The Gospel is John 1:35-39 in which the Baptist hails Jesus as the 'Lamb of God who takes away the sins of the world'. In the Gospel of John, this passage has a link to John 19:14 where it is indicated that the trial of Jesus before Pilate took place on the preparation day for the Passover. That was when the Passover lambs which were to be eaten at the feast were slaughtered in the temple. This thread of the Lamb of God is written into the overall plan of John's Gospel.

3. The symbolism of the Lamb of God. This is an image with many points of reference. Its principal point of reference was the lamb of the Passover which referred to the blood of the lamb with which the doors of the Israelite houses in Egypt were marked in order to save them from the death of the firstborn. Those whose doors were so marked were saved from death.

But this occurs very differently with the Lamb of the New Testament 'whose blood consecrates the homes of all believers' (*The Exsultet*). Jesus, the Lamb of God, is himself led to the slaughter – in the image of Isaiah's lamb (Isaiah 53:7-10). He is the defenceless one who goes to his death so that we may not be subject to death. It is he who bore our sufferings, he who carried our sorrows and who redeemed us from death and sin. (See pages 100–102 in this book).

4. The Awakening of Conscience is based on Psalm 139. The Litany of Prayer is mainly based on Isaiah 52:13 to 53:12. The Prayer used in the Acknowledgment of Sin comes from *The Rite of Penance*, no. 45 (91). The Opening Prayer is the Prayer for the Saturday after Ash Wednesday. The Prayer of Thanksgiving is adapted from those given in the *Rite of Penance*,[57] specifically the one on page 36, no. 57 with the number (208) beside it.

---

[57] *Rite of Penance*. Issued by authority of the Australian Episcopal Conference. Sydney/Melbourne: E. J. Dwyer, 1975.

THE CELEBRATION

ENTRANCE HYMN

INTRODUCTION

OPENING PRAYER

Father, look upon our weakness
and reach out to help us with your loving power.
Through Christ our Lord
All: Amen.

LITURGY OF THE WORD

First Reading: Isaiah 53:2-7
Responsorial Psalm: Psalm 30:2, 15-17, 23
   Response: Into your hands I commend my spirit.
Gospel: John 1:35-39
Homily
Time of Silence

AWAKENING OF CONSCIENCE

Introduction: We come before the Lord who knows us better than we know ourselves. In that spirit, we pray for his light to see our true selves. Above all, we specifically entrust our sinfulness into his hands.
Leader: Lord, you search me and you know me; you know my resting and my rising.
Response: Lord, search me and know me.
Leader: Lord, you know all my ways through and through.

Response: Lord, you search me and you know me.

Leader: Before a word is on my tongue, you know it, Lord.

Response: Lord, you search me and you know me.

Leader: Your hand is ever laid upon me. Too wonderful this knowledge, too high beyond my reach.

Response: Lord, you search me and you know me.

Leader: If I were to take the wings of the dawn or dwell at the sea's furthest end, even there your right hand would hold me fast.

Response: Lord, you search me and you know me.

Leader: My frame was not hidden from you when I was being fashioned in secret and moulded in the depths of the earth.

Response: Lord, you search me and you know me.

Leader: O search me, Lord, and know my heart. Test me and know my thoughts and lead me in the way of eternity.

Response: Lord, you search me and you know me.

PRAYER

Shed your clear light on our hearts, Lord, that walking continually in your way, we may

never separate ourselves from you. We pray this
through Christ our Lord.

All: Amen.

Litany of Prayer

Response to each phrase is 'Lord, have mercy'.

Lord Jesus, you were shunned and despised by
the people.

Lord Jesus, you were familiar with suffering.

Lord Jesus, you were held to be of no account.

Lord Jesus, you bore the sorrows of human
beings.

Lord Jesus, you were brought low by human
power.

Lord Jesus, your wounds brought us healing.

Lord Jesus, you gather all who stray.

Lord Jesus, you were silent before your tormentors.

Lord Jesus, you were like a lamb led to the
slaughter.

Lord Jesus, you were cut off from the land of the
living.

Lord Jesus, you gave your life for us and for all.

Lord Jesus, you are the lamb slain but standing.

Lord Jesus, you take away the sin of the world.

Lord Jesus, you bring us God's peace.

Lord Jesus, you exposed yourself to death and
brought it to an end.

Lord Jesus, you are risen out of death.

Acknowledgment of Sin

Leader (*after a time of silence*)

Together, let us acknowledge our sinfulness in the following prayer.:

All: Lord Jesus Christ, you are the Lamb of God; you take away the sin of the world. Through the grace of the Holy Spirit, restore me to friendship with your Father, cleanse me from every sin through the blood you shed for me and raise me to new life for the glory of your name. Amen. (Rite of Penance[58], p. 25)

Symbolic Action

All move towards the principal crucifix of the church, singing repeatedly a version of the 'Lamb of God' as used at Mass. As people come near to the crucifix, they bow before it.

As they return, they go to the priest/leader and a receive a laying on of hands as a sign of the redemption and reconciliation they have received through Jesus, the Lamb of God.

Prayer of Thanksgiving

Lord God, creator and ruler of your kingdom of light,
in your great love for this world,

---

[58] *Rite of Penance*. Issued by authority of the Australian Episcopal Conference. Sydney/Melbourne: E. J. Dwyer, 1975.

you gave up your only Son for our salvation.
His cross has redeemed us, his death has given us life,
his resurrection has raised us to glory.
Through him we ask you to be always present in the midst of your family.
All: Amen.

BLESSING

DISMISSAL

RECESSIONAL HYMN

CELEBRATION 2
Recognising our sinfulness

Notes for the Celebration

1. The focus of the celebration – if conducted during Lent – could be a prominent placement of the ashes left over from Ash Wednesday. Ashes have been part of the symbolism of repentance from Old Testament times. They remind us of our creation from the dust of the earth and the life-giving breath of God. We acknowledge that we are but dust but that the breath of God has been breathed into us. Christ breathed the breath of life onto his disciples after the resurrection and continues to breathe it into us now.

2. The Awakening of Conscience comes from words on a plaque in the ruins of Coventry Cathedral. It recalls the terrors of war but also a rising from the ashes epitomised in the rebuilding of the new Cathedral.

3. The Litany of Prayer consists of phrases taken from the weekday Collects of Lent.

4. The Opening Prayer is the second form of the one for Ash Wednesday in the earlier English translation of the Roman Missal. The Prayer of Thanksgiving can be found in the *Rite of Penance*,[59] p. 37, no. 57 (211).

---

[59] *Rite of Penance*. Issued by authority of the Australian Episcopal Conference. Sydney/Melbourne: E. J. Dwyer, 1975.

THE CELEBRATION

ENTRANCE HYMN

INTRODUCTION

OPENING PRAYER

Father in heaven,
the light of your truth bestows sight to the
darkness of sinful eyes.
May this celebration of repentance
bring us the blessing of your forgiveness and the
gift of your light.
Through Christ our Lord.
All: Amen.

LITURGY OF THE WORD

First Reading: 2 Samuel 12:1-10 (David and
Nathan)
Responsorial Psalm: Psalm 50:3-6, 18-19
    Response: A humble contrite heart, O God,
you will not spurn
Gospel: John 8:1-11
Homily
Time of Silence

AWAKENING OF CONSCIENCE

We hold before the Lord the instances of human
sinfulness named on a plaque within the ruins
of Coventry Cathedral.
Leader: All have sinned and have come short of
the glory of God.

Response: Lord, have mercy.

Leader: The hatred that divides nation from nation, race from race, class from class.

Response: Lord, have mercy.

Leader: The covetous desires of people and of nations.

Response: Lord, have mercy.

Leader: The greed that exploits the labours of people and lays waste the earth.

Response: Lord, have mercy.

Leader: Our envy of the welfare and happiness of others.

Response: Lord, have mercy.

Leader: Our indifference to the plight of the homeless and the refugee.

Response:Lord, have mercy.

Leader: The lust that uses for ignoble purposes the bodies and women and men.

Response:Lord, have mercy..

Leader: The pride that leads us to trust in ourselves and not in God.

Response: Lord, have mercy.

Leader: Lord, lead us to be kind and tender hearted and forgiving of one another as you have been kind, tender hearted and forgiving of us. Through Christ our Lord.

All: Amen..

LITANY OF PRAYER

Response to each phrase is 'Lord be merciful'.

Lord Jesus, we come before you acknowledging our guilt.
Lord Jesus, look with compassion on our frailty.
Lord Jesus, stretch out your hand to strengthen us.
Lord Jesus, in your gentle mercy, guide our wayward hearts.
Lord Jesus, turn our hearts to you.
Lord Jesus, make our faith eager and strong.
Lord Jesus, kindle in our hearts the fire of your Spirit.
Lord Jesus, your Spirit sets us on the path to life.
Lord Jesus, shed your clear light on our hearts.
Lord Jesus, keep us faithful to our baptism.
Lord Jesus, may we draw the breath of life from your death and Resurrection.

Leader (*after a time of silence*)

Let us acknowledge our sinfulness in the traditional prayer, the Confiteor:

All: I confess to almighty God, and to you, my brothers and sisters,
that I have sinned through my own fault,
in my thoughts and in my words,
in what I have done, and what I have failed to do;
and I ask blessed Mary ever-virgin, all the angels and saints,
and you, my brothers and sisters,
to pray for me to the Lord our God.

SYMBOLIC ACTION

The refrain 'Jesus, remember me' is sung as the people come to the priest/leader for a laying on of hands accompanied by the absolution formula used in the Penitential Rite at Mass:

'May Almighty God have mercy on us, forgive us our sins and bring us to everlasting life'

OR

Using the same refrain, all present could come to the bowl of ashes and sprinkle ashes on their heads as a sign of repentance.

PRAYER OF THANKSGIVING

God and Father of us all,
you have forgiven our sins and sent us your peace.
Help us to forgive one another
and to work together to establish peace in the world.
We pray this through Christ our Lord.
All: Amen.

BLESSING

DISMISSAL

RECESSIONAL HYMN

CELEBRATION 3
The Prodigal Father

Notes for the Celebration

1. The suggested focus of the celebration is the Baptismal Font with the Paschal Candle near it. In baptism, we were claimed for Christ and given a deposit on the future kingdom that we will inherit. In baptism, we receive the bounty of the Prodigal Father and we begin our life journey with Christ who will take us on his passover through life and death to the resurrection.

It is significant that once someone is baptised, that baptism is never repeated. This is so because of the fidelity of God; once God has claimed us as his own, his attitude does not change however much human attitudes may.

2. As background to this celebration, see pages 122–128.

3. The Acknowledgment of Sin and the Litany of Prayer are both based on the beatitudes in Matthew's Gospel. The Beatitudes name qualities in human beings that manifest the blessing of God at work in them and so it is that we seek to see such qualities in ourselves, and in others.

4. The Opening Prayer is that of Friday of the Fourth Week of Lent in the earlier translation of the Roman Missal. The *Prayer of Thanksgiving* is taken from the *Rite of Penance*,[60] p. 35, no. 57.

---

[60] *Rite of Penance.* Issued by authority of the Australian Episcopal Conference. Sydney/Melbourne: E. J. Dwyer, 1975.

THE CELEBRATION

ENTRANCE HYMN

INTRODUCTION

OPENING PRAYER

Father, our source of life, you know our weakness.
May we reach out with joy to grasp your hand
and walk more readily in your ways.
Through Christ our Lord.
All: Amen.

LITURGY OF THE WORD

First Reading: Isaiah 41:8-10, 13-24
Responsorial Psalm: Psalm 130:1-8.
   Response: I will leave this place and go to my
Father
Gospel: Luke 15:11-32
Homily
Time of Silence

AWAKENING OF CONSCIENCE

Introduction: Let us begin by spending a few
minutes 'counting our blessings' and looking at
our gratitude for and fidelity to those blessings.
Then we proceed to awaken our conscience in
terms of the blessings that are recounted in the
Beatitudes given in Matthew's Gospel.

(*Let there be a time of quiet for about 20 seconds
between each beatitude.*)

Blessed are the poor in spirit
  - they know their need of God and of others.
Blessed are the gentle
  - they do not seek to dominate or manipulate.
Blessed are those who mourn
  - they know what it is to love.
Blessed are those who hunger and thirst for justice
  - they know that the world is not as it ought to be.
Blessed are the merciful
  - in them mercy has the last word.
Blessed are the pure in heart
  - goodness is apparent in them.
Blessed are the peacemakers
  - they go beyond the divisions that afflict human beings.
Blessed are those who are persecuted in the cause of right
  - they live out their faith at a cost.

Prayer: Lord, may your ever-present blessings flourish and bear fruit in your people as they turn to you, acknowledging their sinfulness. We pray this through Christ our Lord.
All: Amen.

LITANY OF PRAYER
Each petition is followed by the response 'Lord, have mercy'.

Lord Jesus, you gather the poor of spirit into your kingdom.

Lord Jesus, you give the gentle their inheritance.
Lord Jesus, you give comfort to those in sorrow.
Lord Jesus, you will nourish those who hunger
and thirst for justice.
Lord Jesus, you show the depths of your mercy
to the merciful.
Lord Jesus, you promise the pure of heart that
they shall see God.
Lord Jesus, you make peacemakers true children of
God.
Lord Jesus, you promise to those who seek
justice that they will have the kingdom of God.

ACKNOWLEDGMENT OF SIN

Leader (*after a time of silence*)

Let us acknowledge our sinfulness using the
following prayer:

All: Father of mercy, like the prodigal son I
return to you and say:
I have sinned against you and am not worthy to
be called your child.
Christ Jesus, I pray with the repentant thief:
Lord, remember me in your kingdom.
Holy Spirit, fountain of love, I call on you with trust:
purify my heart, help me to walk as a child of the
light.
(*Rite of Penance*[61], no. 45, [88])

---

[61] *Rite of Penance*. Issued by authority of the Australian Episcopal Conference.
Sydney/Melbourne: E. J. Dwyer, 1975.

SYMBOLIC ACTION

While singing 'Jesus, remember me' (or some other suitable hymn), all approach the priest/leader, who signs them on the forehead with a cross, saying:

In your baptism, you were claimed for Christ by the sign of his cross. May you be always faithful to the Lord who has claimed you as his own.

PRAYER OF THANKSGIVING

Almighty and merciful Father,
you do not abandon sinners, but seek them out
with a Father's love.
You sent your Son into the world to destroy sin
and death and to restore life and joy.
You sent the Holy Spirit into our hearts to make
us your children and heirs to your kingdom.
We thank you for the wonders of your mercy
and join in your Church's song of praise:
Glory to you through Christ in the Holy Spirit,
now and forever.
All: Amen. Amen.

BLESSING

DISMISSAL

RECESSIONAL HYMN

SUGGESTED HYMNS

(GA = Gather Australia; CWB = Catholic Worship Book)

	GA	CWB
As gentle as silence		580
A trusting psalm	455	293
Be merciful, O Lord (Psalm 51)	61	92
Be with me, Lord (Psalm 91)	53	286
Come as you are	212	
Come back to me (Hosea)	213	
Create in me (Psalm 51)	40	478
God of mercy and compassion	302	290
Grant to us, O Lord	303	291
How rich are the depths of God (Psalm 139)	81	505
I have loved you	402	511
I put my life in your hands (Psalm 31)	30	
Jesus, remember me	308	526
Micah's theme	486	
My soul is longing for your peace	519	559
O God, you search me and you know me		572
O Jesus crucified	334	326
Seek, O seek the Lord	211	595
The lord is kind and merciful (Psalm 103)	61	
To you, O Lord (Psalm 25)	26	632
Yes, I shall arise	214	648